Rolling Out 5G

Use Cases, Applications, and Technology Solutions

Biljana Badic
Christian Drewes
Ingolf Karls
Markus Mueck

Apress®

Rolling Out 5G: Use Cases, Applications, and Technology Solutions

Biljana Badic
Intel Deutschland GmbH, Munich, Germany

Christian Drewes
Intel Deutschland GmbH, Munich, Germany

Ingolf Karls
Intel Deutschland GmbH, Munich, Germany

Markus Mueck
Intel Deutschland GmbH, Munich, Germany

ISBN-13 (pbk): 978-1-4842-1507-4
DOI 10.1007/978-1-4842-1506-7

ISBN-13 (electronic): 978-1-4842-1506-7

Library of Congress Control Number: 2016942100

Managing Director: Welmoed Spahr
Lead Editor: James DeWolf
Development Editor: James Markham
Technical Reviewer: Eryk Dutciewicz, Beeshanga Abewardana Jayawickrama, and Diep N. Nguyen
Editorial Board: Steve Anglin, Pramila Balen, Louise Corrigan, James DeWolf, Jonathan Gennick, Robert Hutchinson, Celestin Suresh John, Nikhil Karkal, James Markham, Susan McDermott, Matthew Moodie, Douglas Pundick, Ben Renow-Clarke, Gwenan Spearing
Coordinating Editor: Melissa Maldonado
Copy Editor: James A. Compton
Compositor: SPi Global
Indexer: SPi Global
Artist: SPi Global

Distributed to the book trade worldwide by Springer Science+Business Media New York, 233 Spring Street, 6th Floor, New York, NY 10013. Phone 1-800-SPRINGER, fax (201) 348-4505, e-mail orders-ny@springer-sbm.com, or visit www.springer.com. Apress Media, LLC is a California LLC and the sole member (owner) is Springer Science + Business Media Finance Inc (SSBM Finance Inc). SSBM Finance Inc is a **Delaware** corporation.

For information on translations, please e-mail rights@apress.com, or visit www.apress.com.

Apress and friends of ED books may be purchased in bulk for academic, corporate, or promotional use. eBook versions and licenses are also available for most titles. For more information, reference our Special Bulk Sales–eBook Licensing web page at www.apress.com/bulk-sales.

Any source code or other supplementary materials referenced by the author in this text is available to readers at www.apress.com. For detailed information about how to locate your book's source code, go to www.apress.com/source-code/.

Printed on acid-free paper

Contributors: Thorsten Clevorn, Michael Faerber, Stefan Franz, Alexander Maltsev, Bernhard Raaf, Srikathyayani Srikanteswara

Contents at a Glance

Contents

About the Authors

Dr. Biljana Badic works at Intel in Munich, focusing on the development, architecture evolution and performance optimization of Intel cellular modems. She has been also actively involved in Intel research activities on 4G and 5G systems. Prior to joining Intel in 2010, Biljana was a Senior Reseacher at the School of Engineering, Swansea University, UK, where she worked on the design of energy-efficient radio access architecture for WWANs, and from 2002 to 2006 Biljana was employed as Research and Teaching Assistant at the Institute for Communications and Radio-Frequency Engineering, Vienna University of Technology, where she worked on research of multiple systems and space-time codes. Biljana received her Dipl.-Ing. Degree in electrical engineering and information technology from the Graz University of Technology, Austria in 1996 and Dr. –Tech. degree from the Vienna University of Technology in 2005. She has published more than fifty scientific articles and filed more than twenty 4G patents.

Dr. Christian Drewes works at Intel in Munich on system architecture and innovation across the cellular product portfolio. A special focus is on end-user aspects like data throughput and power consumption. Within those activities, Christian and his team contribute to cellular platform productization, grounding knowledge with field experience, and guiding future cellular platform architectures. In addition, Christian teaches as a guest lecturer at the Technical University of Munich. Christian grew up in the Munich area and received Dipl.-Ing. and Dr.-Ing. degrees in electrical engineering and information technology from the Technical University of Munich, Germany. He started his industry career at Infineon Technologies in 2000, and joined Intel with the acquisition of Infineon's Wireless Group in 2011.

Dr. Ingolf Karls works at Intel Deutschland GmbH in the Communication and Devices Group. He got his Master and PhD degree at Technical University Chemnitz. After that he contributed to the second, third, and fourth generations of mobile communication systems at Siemens AG, Infineon Technologies AG, and Intel. He fostered partnerships between wireless ecosystem stakeholders as an active member of national and international regulation and standardization bodies like 3GPP, BITKOM, DLNA, ETSI, IEEE, ITU and OMA. He has consulted for Germany's BMBF, BMWi and European Commission on wireless communication technologies. He currently works on fifth-generation mobile communication millimeter wave topics like spectrum regulation, channel models, access and front and backhaul techniques as part of next-generation networking and is program manager for 3GPP standardization at Intel.

Dr. Markus Mueck oversees Intel's technology development, standardization and partnerships in the field of spectrum sharing. In this capacity, he has contributed to standardization and regulatory efforts on various topics including spectrum sharing within numerous industry standards bodies, including ETSI, 3GPP, IEEE, the Wireless Innovation Forum and CEPT. Dr. Mueck is an adjunct professor of engineering at Macquarie University, Sydney. He acts as an ETSI Board Member supported by INTEL and as general Chairman of ETSI RRS Technical Body (Software Radio and Cognitive Radio Standardization). He has earned engineering degrees from the University of Stuttgart, Germany, and the Ecole Nationale Supérieure des Télécommunications (ENST) in Paris, as well as a doctorate degree of ENST in Communications. From 1999 to 2008, Dr. Mueck was Senior Staff member and Technical Manager at Motorola Labs, Paris. In this role, he contributed actively to various standardization bodies,including Digital Radio Mondiale, IEEE 802.11n, and led the creation of the novel standardization group IEEE P1900.4 in the area of Cognitive Radio and Software Defined Radio (SDR). He also contributed to numerous European Research projects, namely as Technical Manager of IST-E2R II (19 MEuros budget) and as overall technical leader for the definition of IST-E3 (20 MEuros budget).

About the Technical Reviewers

Dr. Eryk Dutkiewicz received his B.E. degree in Electrical and Electronic Engineering from the University of Adelaide, Australia, in 1988, his M.Sc. degree in Applied Mathematics from the University of Adelaide in 1992 and his PhD in Telecommunications from the University of Wollongong, Australia, in 1996. His industry experience includes management of the Wireless Research Laboratory at Motorola in the early 2000s. He is currently the Head of School of Computing and Communications at the University of Technology Sydney. He has held visiting professorial appointments at several institutions, including the Chinese Academy of Sciences, Shanghai JiaoTong University and Macquarie University. His current research interests cover 5G networks and medical body area networks.

Dr. Diep N. Nguyen is a faculty member of the School of Computing and Communications, University of Technology Sydney (UTS). He received M.E. and Ph.D. in Electrical and Computer Engineering from University of California, San Diego (UCSD) and The University of Arizona (UA), respectively. Before joining UTS, he was a DECRA Research Fellow at Macquarie University, a member of technical staff at Broadcom (California), and ARCON Corporation (Boston), and he consulted forthe Federal Aviation Administration (FAA)on turning detection of UAVs and aircraft, and for the US Air Force on anti-jamming, as a postdoctoral scientist at the University of Arizona. He has received several awards from LG Electronics, University of California at San Diego, The University of Arizona, the National Science Foundation (US), and the Australian Research Council, including the Best Paper award finalist at the WiOpt conference (2014), and the Discovery Early Career Researcher award (DECRA, 2015). His recent research interests are in the areas of computer networking, wireless communications, and machine learning, with an emphasis on systems' performance and security/privacy.

Dr. Beeshanga Abewardana Jayawickrama received a BEng degree in telecommunications engineering and Ph.D. degree in electronic engineering from Macquarie University, Sydney, in 2011 and 2015 respectively.

Following his Ph.D. he held a Research Associate position in the Department of Engineering at Macquarie University. He is currently a Lecturer in the School of Computing and Communications, University of Technology Sydney. His research interests are resource allocation in wireless networks, cognitive radio, compressed sensing, and cross-layer techniques.

Acknowledgments

The authors would like to express their gratitude to Intel Corporation and in particular to Prof. Dr. Josef Hausner for supporting this book project.

In no particular order and with no implication of the importance of their contributions to the book, we thank the following colleagues:

Thorsten Clevorn, Michael Faerber, Stefan Franz, Alexander Maltsev, Bernhard Raaf, Srikathyayani Srikanteswara, and Geng Wu for their efforts to substantially improve the quality of this book and make it useful to a broad audience.

Foreword

Few books combine both the theoretical essentials and the practical realities of radio systems engineering, but the authors have really hit both of those goals at once. This is both a critical reference book on 4G's evolution and a practical guide to the 5G vectors that industry is exploring. 5G is like a football game with seven or eight teams on the field at once where there are many nets but only one goal worth scoring: minimum CAPEX and OPEX for maximum 5G use-case capability. It is an elusive target, for which this new book is the perfect guide.

The retrospective of Chapter 1 sets the stage, looking back to 1G and forward to 5G, presented with uncanny insight into use cases, business, and technology ecosystems.

Chapter 2 shows how semiconductor technology has adapted to the challenges, clearly delineating the factors driving radio access network and packet core evolution, including radio interference management, interference mitigation and network-assistance: the goal is always the end-user experience.

Chapter 3 is a great tutorial on the forces competing to evolve 4G into 5G; the crucial role of RAN densification looms large.

Chapter 4 honestly states that we just don't know which technologies will define 5G, but the contenders include shared spectrum and millimeter wave bands, orchestrated by increased context awareness.

Chapter 5 then digs into the variety of spectrum-sharing paradigms being developed for eventual mass markets globally.

The authors save the best for last, with a comprehensive treatment of the potential and myriad challenges of the centimeter and millimeter wave bands.

Key topics are developed throughout, such as network function virtualization and the software-defined Internet of Things, including V2X and self-driving cars. Of course as the "Godfather" of software-defined and cognitive radio, I make it my business to stay abreast of these developments, so I can guarantee you this book has a special place not on my bookshelf, but on my desk and in my briefcase as an essential pocket guide to 5G.

Dr. Joseph Mitola III, Mitola's STATISfaction
President and CEO, Hackproof Technologies Inc.

CHAPTER 1

Introduction to Mobile Wireless Systems

Contributor: Michael Faerber

The evolution of wireless systems has taken place in a remarkably short time, delivering incredible technology advances that have changed the way people communicate and interact with each other. Those advances have come in several generations; the mobile wireless communication journey started with 1G, followed by 2G, 3G, 4G, and now 5G, the standard currently under specification. Each generation of wireless systems followed different evolutionary paths toward two unified targets: delivering greater performance and efficiency, and doing so in highly complex network deployments.

A more advanced technology will address escalating demand and provide higher performance, but at the same time it will create new usage models and increase demand even further. For example, LTE network operators reported over 150 percent data increase over 3G consumption, up to 46 MB per day from 17 MB per day [1]. This trend will continue with 5G and later. New technologies are creating new demand and applications, as shown in Figure 1-1. Very often, it is not even clear what kind of applications will be requested by users when a new technology is introduced. Similarly, users might initially not know what basic capabilities a new technology enables. This closed-loop feedback circle between end-users, applications, devices, and technology can lead to a self-energizing circle of innovation. As a result of this virtuous circle, peak data rates of cellular systems have doubled every 18 months in the last decades since the introduction of the first digital 2G phones, and no end is in sight.

© Intel Corp. 2016
B. Badic et al., *Rolling Out 5G*, DOI 10.1007/978-1-4842-1506-7_1

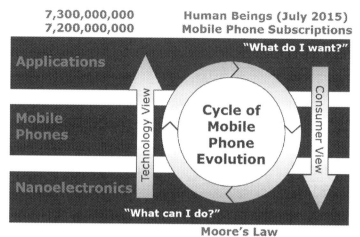

Figure 1-1. *Cycle of mobile phone evolution*

Why do we need a succession of generations of wireless standards? Why, every decade, are all investments in the old generation scraped away and massive costs and engineering efforts put into the development of the new one? It is obvious; the evolution of wireless systems is an endless process. People need to communicate, and being connected all the time is now the basic assumption and natural fabric of everyday life. *New technologies are about how people meet, express ideas and communicate, define identities, and understand each other. Being connected is a way of life.* Wireless communication has become a fundamental element of today's economy, supporting entire industries and impacting not only how people work, but how they live their lives.

Wireless Evolution: a Retrospective

The first handheld mobile cell phone was produced by Motorola in 1973. Prior to that, mobile telephony was used only in vehicles. The prototype handheld phones weighed 1.1 kg and measured 23 cm long, 13 cm deep and 4.45 cm wide. You could talk for just 30 minutes, and it took 10 hours to recharge the battery [2]. The first commercial cellular network was launched by NTT in Japan in 1979, followed in 1981 by the Nordic Mobile Telephone (NMT) system in Denmark, Finland, Norway, and Sweden. And the development of mobile wireless communication had begun. The first generation (1G) mobile wireless communication network, launched in the 80s, was analog cellular technology and supported voice calls only. The second generation (2G), available in the 90s, used a digital technology and supported text messaging and lower-speed data. The third generation (3G), which became available in the last decade, provided multimedia support along with higher data transmission rates and increased capacity. After almost 10 years of 3G development, it had become clear that 3G networks could not keep up with the tremendous growth of applications requiring high bandwidth and data rates; as a consequence, the development of the fourth generation (4G) has started.

The first two commercially available technologies referred to as 4G were the WiMAX standard (offered in the U.S. by Sprint) and the LTE offered in Scandinavia by TeliaSonera. The key difference between 4G and its predecessors is its elimination of circuit-switching and instead employing an all-IP network; that is, voice calls are established using packet-switching over Internet, LAN, or WAN networks via VoIP just like any other type of streaming audio media.

Currently, standardization bodies have started to define the fifth generation (5G). It is expected that 5G will bring a real wireless world—the Wireless World Wide Web(WWWW)—supporting enormous data rates and huge numbers of user applications and services. Even though it is not yet clear what 5G will be, research institutions have started looking into the sixth (6G) and seventh (7G) generations of wireless systems, proposing to integrate satellite networks and to introduce space roaming in future wireless generations.

Wireless Generations in a Nutshell

Table 1-1 summarizes wireless cellular standards from 1G to 5G, and Figure 1-2 shows how the data rate increases over wireless generations.

Table 1-1. *Evolution of Wireless Standards*

Standard	1G	2G	2.5G	3G	3.5G	4G	5G
Launch	1981	1991	2001	2001	2006	2009	2020
Access technology	e.g. AMPS, NMT	GSM, D-AMPS	GPRS, EDGE, CDMA	CDMA 2000 WCDMA TDSCDMA	HSPA EVDO	LTE, WiMAX	Different air interface variants (AIV)
Encoding	Analog	Digital	Digital	Digital	Digital	Digital	Digital
Date rate (per user) on average	4.8kbps	64kbps	144kbps	384 kbps	>2Mbps Peak: 42 Mbps or even 63 Mbps,	1Gbps	>1Gbps
Service	Voice only	Digital voice, SMS	Voice, SMS, MMS	Integrated audio, video and data	Integrated audio, video and data	Dynamic data access, IoT, Voice over VoLTE	Broadband access everywhere, massive IoT, extreme real-time communication, ultra-reliable communication
Switching	Circuit	Circuit, Packet	Packet	Packet Circuit,	All packet	All packet	All packet

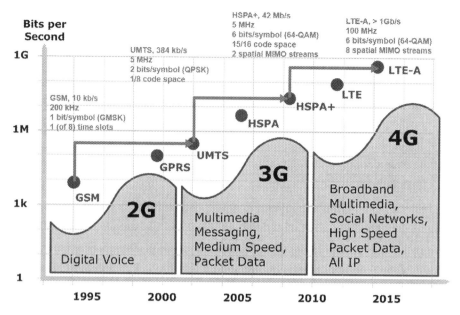

Figure 1-2. *Wireless generations and corresponding data rates*

From Analog Voice to High Data Rate and Multiple Services in Parallel

The first generation of cellular systems was analog cellular technology, supporting voice only. The voice transmission was made by narrowband FM transmission in FDMA-FDD (Frequency Domain Multiple Access Frequency Division Duplex). Signalling was based on low-rate binary FSK (Frequency Shift Keying) signalling, control mechanisms were mainly network-centric, and signalling mostly consisted of downlinks. Because the voice is an analog phenomenon, analog modulation is the most straightforward method, with the least number of intermediate steps and no need for any buffer or storage, which is difficult to implement in analog technology.

A major shortcoming of the 1G systems was the lack of security. The FM transmission could be easily eavesdropped and besides listening to the conversation, the signalling messages could be tapped. This allowed intruders to do things like read a user's identity. Typically user and terminal were considered identical, and fraud was easy. Another shortcoming of 1G mobile systems was that the handover procedures had been based on field strength measurements of the base stations. In networks with an increasing traffic density, the downlink-controlled handover procedure required high re-use distances and thus reduced the spectral efficiency. The other clear shortcoming of 1G systems was that roaming was not possible; even when a system like NMT was used in Austria, a Swedish user couldn't use his phone abroad [2].

2G introduced digital processing and TDMA (Time Division Multiplexing Access). In this system the modulation was digital; audio signals were compressed by digital algorithms before transmission, typically processing the speech signal in blocks. Furthermore, it introduced encryption, and roaming was a must. Network infrastructure was getting more efficient, comprising eight traffic channels on a 200 kHz carrier. For the terminal, the standard makers made a big bet on the progress of signal processing, higher integration of functions, and a common market providing an economy of scale.

2.5G introduced CDMA (Code Division Multiple Access) transmission technology to mobile cellular networks in USA. The origin of the concept stems from Qualcomm; thus it was initially a proprietary concept, which received support by some operators, and then became a US standard. The concept was later known alternatively as IS-95 or CDMA.

Common to all 2G systems is a single service (voice) and *Short message service (SMS)*. Later, the General Packet Radio Service (GPRS) introduced the packet-switched (PS) domain to mobile network architectures. GPRS featured different modulation and coding schemes (MCS), but it lacked a practical automatic link adaptation. Packet scheduling had been introduced, as well as sharing the same radio resource for a multiplicity of users, but the available data rates still remained quite low. Time slot concatenation was introduced, but practical terminal implementations did not use the theoretically possible maximum rates. So in the second half of the 90s, work on EDGE (Enhanced Data Rates for GSM Evolution) was started. EDGE introduced a new modulation format to the GSM concept, to enable higher data rates under good radio conditions. It also features an automatic link adaptation, adjusting the MCS to the channel quality. HARQ (Hybrid Automatic Repeat Request) schemes had been introduced as well. Using the new modulation scheme and timeslot concatenation, the 2G system was able to provide serious data rates for the first time [2].

3G remained digital, but intended to increase peak data rates significantly compared to 2G. This was only possible by using more frequency bandwidth and higher symbol rates. Therefore CDMA was introduced, together with the *rake receiver*, a new kind of equalizer, easy to implement with simple operations (just add and subtract). With Release 5 the HSDPA (High Speed Downlink Packet Access) concept became part of the standard, which introduced important technical enhancements for data service support in downlink. In Release 6, improvements for the UL were introduced (HSUPA, High Speed Uplink Packet Access), which turned the WCDMA into high speed packet access (HSPA). Voice and video were kept on the DCH (downlink channel), but HSPA enabled efficient provision of packet data over the 3G air interface.

WiMAX and LTE, the Path Toward 4G

Work on 4G started in the mid-2000s. ITU was calling for another deadline to define more advanced requirements, called IMT-Advanced, and with the accumulated experience from 3G, the idea emerged to design a system concept for IMT. Another push came from the emergence of WiMAX (Worldwide Interoperability for Microwave Access), an IEEE (Institute of Electrical and Electronics Engineers) standard activity. IEEE and the WiFi certification group continuously worked and enhanced the WLAN (wireless local area network) standard, freeing users from connecting computers and notebooks by cables to a LAN. Logically, this leads to the idea of evolving this successful technology to wide-area usage. It is worth noting that WiMAX has a suite of solutions, many involving wireless backhaul. Only one variant was a mobile WiMAX, but this mobile version is today most often what is referred to as WiMAX.

WiMAX emerged from the IEEE world, it was based on a different network architecture than 3GPP, and it introduced a new air interface, OFDMA (Orthogonal Frequency Division Multiple Access). Many network operators had been frustrated by the complexity of operating a 3G system and were happy to see a fresh approach. The 3GPP community realized the threat coming from this competing technology, and this accelerated the work on the 3G evolution and removed barriers to acceptance of many new features and architectures. A flat architecture was seen as a must, removing the Radio Network Controller (RNC) as well as the Base Station Controller (BSC) entity from the RAN; the circuit-switched domain was given up, as all services use the packet-switched domain. MIMO (Multiple Input Multiple Output) and multi antenna support in the UE (User Equipment) were key requirements, along with simplified channel structures and a state engine, which were finally leading to huge enhancements in the peak rates.

This concept was now called Long Term Evolution (LTE). To avoid the impression of a disruption to 3G, the term 4G was avoided in the beginning. WiMAX served in that phase as a very efficient incubator (almost a blueprint) for the LTE design, but it failed to get a foothold in the 3GPP standardization and did not influence the global standard itself. There was an attempt to promote WiMAX as the TDD (Time Division Duplex) solution for LTE. However, in 3G the TDD development was dominated by Chinese organizations, and there was little willingness to leave this field to a different community. Eventually, the attempt to align the numerologies of the emerging LTE FDD and a WiMAX TDD may have come too late. LTE uplink was decided to be based on SC-FDMA (Single Carrier FDMA) for PAPR (Peak-to-Average Power Ratio) reasons, but politically it raised the bar for WiMAX to make its way into a 3GPP standard.

OFDMA was used instead of CDMA, because the rake receiver became less efficient for the highest data rates and because OFDMA allows picking the best frequencies for a user's signal to support both time- and frequency-domain scheduling. The former had already been introduced in HSDPA, and there had even been attempts to use OFDMA in conjunction with UMTS, but in the end it was felt that the advantages of OFDM wouldn't justify a complex, hybrid system.

WiMAX made its market attempts but did not manage to grow into a relevant size. CDMA2000 lost connection to the 4G evolution, when key companies removed their experts from the 3GPP2 standards group and moved them to 3GPP.

This creates the situation we have today, where the dominant standards group is 3GPP and the pacemaking standard is LTE including LTE-Advanced. The lack of competition can create a kind of comfort zone, which may have a negative impact on technical evolution. Competition and ITU deadlines have called for decisions about what is part of a release or not. 3GPP faces the risk of slowing down, developing endless ramifications and too-large functional steps.

A comprehensive summary of each wireless generation can be found in [1].

Device Evolution: Handsets to Smartphones

The first mobile phones were indeed mainly used for making mobile phone calls. The start was made by the first car-phones of the mid-twentieth century, which cost more than the car itself and weighed so much that you could actually only use them in a car while being mobile. Until the early years of the twenty-first century, most innovation went into reducing the size of the phone and extending the lifetime of a single battery charge to multiple weeks.

Usage of the phone changed slightly with the introduction of smartphones. Early smartphones from the end of the twentieth century combined PDA (personal digital assistant) functionality with a mobile phone and supported basic web browsing functionality. In general, smartphones combine phone functionality with generic computing functionality, positioning capability, camera, and all kind of sensors. Third-party applications can be installed via online distribution systems or application stores. Early smartphones usually had a physical keyboard. When touchscreens were introduced roughly a decade ago, they quickly dominated the form-factors of smartphones within a couple of years. Because smartphones are used for many more applications besides telephony, batteries need to be recharged daily.

Social and Economic Aspects and Impacts

A decade ago, early smartphones had a rather small market share, far from dominating the mobile phone market. When Apple released the first iPhone in 2007, the mobile technology with touchscreen technology started, and since then it has revolutionized our lives in ways we barely even notice. And the technology that drives mobile devices has improved a lot since those days. Smartphones have gotten smaller and more powerful, and their number is rapidly increasing, making significant improvements in many lives. *They gave a voice to those without one, and they connected those living in a void; simply said, they brought the whole world closer together.*

The European Commission has recognized this trend and implemented the Digital Single Market (DSM) Strategy [4]. It relies on the three pillars Access, Environment, and Economy & Society. A European DSM is expected to create up to 415 Billion Euros of additional growth and hundreds of thousands of new jobs—in the context of a vibrant knowledge-based society. It is indeed recognized that "Europe needs investment in ICT infrastructures such as cloud computing and Big Data; research and innovation to boost industrial competiveness; and an inclusive society, with better public services and better digital skills for citizens [5]."

Motivation for 4G Evolution

The evolution of mobile phones and cellular radio systems goes hand in hand with the evolution of mobile phone usage, starting from pure voice telephony services, adding messaging, browsing, social networking, and multimedia services. The requirements of those added services include ever-increasing peak data rates, reduced end-to-end service latency, and increased network capacity in terms of data volume and user density. New use cases will evolve according to those dimensions, requiring mobile broadband connectivity (3D video, virtual reality), real-time communications (interactive video, industry control, tactile Internet), massive Internet-of-Things connectivity (sensor networks, smart metering). In addition, use cases will arise using evolved 4G capabilities that are beyond today's usages and potentially even beyond today's imagination, for instance based on the just starting market for wearable devices like smart glasses or smart watches.

Key 5G Enablers

5G is certainly one of the hottest topics in today's fast-evolving mobile wireless ecosystem, and there are debates in almost all market sectors to resolve the uncertainty over what 5G is going to be. Communication ecosystem stakeholders worldwide are now gathering around to discuss and agree upon in details further extensions of the 4G cellular standard and of 5G technology for 2020. The 5G landscape as we know it today changes quickly, its shape driven by the many known and unknown business imperatives. Examples are the extreme mobile broadband (xMBB) and enhanced Machine-to-machine communication (eMTC), both for the Internet of Things. So 2016 will be the year to determine what is hype and what is real, to reach consensus about key features like the new air interface, frame structure, and numerology.

5G extends to an extraordinary degree the exploration of the value of spectrum and how mobile operators and their ecosystem partners deal with it to serve their customers. Hence, a further improvement in spectrum efficiency will be key, adding densification and spectrum sharing to new radio access. New radio access is an imperative key building block of 5G, supporting the xMBB and xMTC use cases. Related to that is another key item, the millimeter wave technology, which has to fulfil the demands of the recent and future rapid growth of extreme broadband wireless applications. And there is the opportunity to define a flexible duplex scheme for devices to transmit within a unified TDD/FDD frame structure and therefore using both modes simultaneously.

Device-to-device (D2D) communication is gaining increasing attention. It is viewed as one more 5G key technology for offloading traffic from networks, improving energy efficiency, and extending coverage. Closely related to it are vehicle-to-vehicle communication, advanced driver assistance systems (ADAS), and autonomous cars, all of which are emerging automotive trends and further becoming an essential part of 5G.

The 5G system will need to scale in many vectors compared to previous wireless network generations. Just to name a few requirements, it must be easy to deploy, scalable, flexible, and cost- and energy-efficient. Therefore heterogeneous networks that include a split between control and user planes play a very important role in 5G systems; they implement concepts of dual and multiple connectivity by using existing and new air interfaces for radio access. Small cells for network densification are another significant 5G aspect, in which the wireless backhaul technology has to provide single- and multi-hop links from fiber to small cell basis stations. Context-aware networking is a key enabler for 5G; it will be needed to increase the overall system efficiency and to provide seamless service delivery and the best user experience at the right time with the right means. Then there are networking and virtualization methods like software-defined networking (SDN), network functions virtualization (NFV), and mobile edge computing (MEC); these, along with centralized network functions, drive a much tighter integration between base stations and enhanced signalling to deliver better network performance. And these methods address the prospect of dynamically created opportunistic networks (ON) as operator-governed, temporary and coordinated extensions of an existing network infrastructure. Open Source Software is expected to play a major role in all of these enablers, adapting generic equipment platforms to the multitude of use cases or enabling the modification of radio parameters in devices. Vertical network slicing will allow to allocate network resources to target vertical applications, to be complemented by horizontal slicing in order to further improve the efficiency of the allocation of available resources across the entire network.

This book answers all these questions about 5G, describing not only 5G's key features as such but also its technical aspects, using the most current information about the rollout of 5G.

Standardization and Regulation Bodies and Their Activities

The standardization and regulation of 5G is a very complex debate, with a wide range of possible options regarding spectrum, technologies, and competing 5G ecosystem stakeholder interests. The standardization and regulation bodies worldwide with significant resources are busy defining 5G roadmaps with input from 4G Americas including USA, 5G Forum Korea, 5GMF Japan, 5G-PPP Europe, and the IMT-2020 5G Promotion Group China.

The most commonly aligned roadmaps are from ITU-R and 3GPP. ITU-R WP5D developed a work plan on spectrum and technology timelines extending to 2020 for 5G. Key dates on the ITU-R IMT-2020 roadmap are the opening for proposal submission as of October 2017, the initial technology submission as of June 2019, and the detailed specification submission as of October 2020. Consequently, 3GPP set up its roadmap to be able to submit final specifications to ITU-R as of February 2020 based on functional specifications frozen as of December 2019. 3GPP started work on 5G in September 2015. The specifications for the next generation of mobile broadband access will come in two phases, where the first phase will be completed in the second half of 2018 (3GPP Release 15) and the second phase will finish by end of 2019 (3GPP Release 16). Still, 3GPP will not be able to address all angles of a highly diverse and heterogeneous 5G system, serving the needs of virtually any imaginable vertical application. ETSI, European Telecommunications Standards Institute, complements the efforts by developing standards in the fields of network function virtualization, mobile edge computing, machine-to-machine communication, cybersecurity, software reconfiguration, and so on. IEEE, on the other hand, is further developing its 802.11 standards collection, enabling in particular next-generation, ultra-high–throughput WiFi and mmWave communication systems.

The ITU World Radio communication Conference 2015 (WRC-15) had around 3300 delegates representing 162 countries and around 500 observers from 130 other entities, including mobile, satellite and broadcasting industries; its results revealed the diverse spectrum interests of different industries, including broadcast, mobile, and wireless communications and satellites. And all of them need to be brought into line globally with incumbent spectrum users, like security services and military, who are using significant parts of spectrum there. One key achievement was a mobile allocation of an additional 709 MHz for IMT at a nearly global scale, for example the largest contiguous range of 200 MHz below 6 GHz between 3400 and 3600 MHz. The conference also saw possible IMT identifications in bands above 6 GHz for IMT-2020 within the 24.25-86 GHz range; these include 24.25-27.5 GHz, 31.8-33.4 GHz, 37-40.5 GHz, 40.5-42.5 GHz, 42.5-43.5 GHz, 45.5-47 GHz, 47-47.2 GHz, 47.2-50.2 GHz, 50.4-52.6 GHz, 66-76 GHz, and 81-86 GHz but exclude 6-24 GHz and 27.5-31.8 GHz.

Looking at 5G use cases and scenarios of the regional fora above, differences show up as well. China is at this time more focused on vertical applications and services. Japan currently favors extreme mobile broadband but supports vertical sectors as well. Korea is mainly focused now on extreme mobile broadband, which is driven by 8K-UHD video. The USA supports an approach similar to the European one, focusing on extreme mobile broadband as well as extreme machine type communication, including vehicle-to-X communication (V2X), where X stands for everything.

References

1. 4G America, "Beyond LTE: Enabling the Mobile Broadband Explosion", White paper, 4G Americas, August 2014.
2. Martin Cooper, et al., "Radio Telephone System", US Patent number 3,906,166; Filing date: 17 October 1973; Issue date: September 1975; Assignee Motorola
3. B. Raaf, M Faerber, B. Badic, V. Frascolla, " Key technology advancements driving mobile communications from generation to generation", Intel Technology Journal, Volume 18, Issue 1, 2014.
4. European Digital Single Market, https://ec.europa.eu/digital-agenda/en/digital-single-market
5. Digital as a driver for growth, Ensuring that Europe's economy, industry and employment take full advantage of what digitalisation offers, European Commission, https://ec.europa.eu/priorities/digital-single-market/digital-driver-growth_en

CHAPTER 2

▓ ▓ ▓

The Evolution and Technology Adaptations of 4G

Contributors: Thorsten Clevorn, Stefan Franz, Bernhard Raaf

This chapter provides a comprehensive view of the challenges facing current 4G networks and how the evolution toward 5G is expected to overcome them. We will explain many of the future requirements that can already be met with LTE Advanced Pro, and we will discuss the operational and implementation challenges in current LTE networks and related end-user experience.

The Growth of 4G

As 4G is the fastest-growing cellular technology, it is expected that mobile operators will continue investing in its development until at least 2020. At the same time, 3GPP continues to further develop 4G standards. In October 2015, the evolving 4G was officially named LTE-Advanced Pro, a name change that starts with the current Release 13 and will continue into future 3GPP releases. LTE-Advanced Pro includes new features such as Licensed-Assisted Access (LAA), 3D beamforming (also known as Full-Dimension MIMO), Narrowband IoT (NB-IoT), Vehicle-to-Everything Communication (V2X), Massive Carrier Aggregation, enhanced Machine Type Communication (eMTC), latency reduction, Downlink Multiuser Superposition Transmission, and Single Cell Point to Multipoint transmission (SC-PTM). The focus of LTE-Advanced Pro is to further improve network capacity and user experience, and to expand the set of supported applications. It will significantly promote LTE technology and at the same time shape current networks toward 5G requirements.

With all these new features to be supported in complex heterogeneous deployments that have increased numbers of users and hence increased interference, it will take years of refining current concepts and techniques to achieve 4G's anticipated performance. With varying data rates, channel characteristics, and different bandwidth allocation and handover support among heterogeneous deployments, maintaining the QoS promised for 4G remains a major challenge in 4G networks deployments.

© Intel Corp. 2016
B. Badic et al., *Rolling Out 5G*, DOI 10.1007/978-1-4842-1506-7_2

Implementation Challenges

The ever-increasing demand for higher data rates is enabled by "Moore's Law," a forecast that the number of components per integrated circuit will double every two years. This forecast was made by Gordon Moore originally in 1965, when he stated that the number components doubled every year, and refined in 1975 to a doubling every two years [1]. This "law" has driven the evolution of micro-electronics over the last 50 years and has enabled the doubling of peak data rates in cellular radio handsets every 18 months, as shown in Figure 2-1.

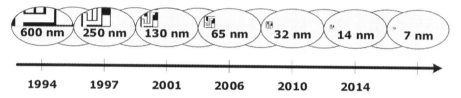

Figure 2-1. *Semiconductor technology nodes as a driving force behind Moore's Law. Moore's Law enables high performance at low cost, current, and size*

Baseband

This increasing peak data rate is reflected in the required chip area. Figure 2-2 compares the relative die sizes of a 2G macro (EGPRS class 34, 300 kbps peak data rate), a 3G macro (HSDPA, 42 Mbps), and an LTE macro (450 Mbps). Main contributors for this macro area are typically PHY processing modules. As expected, chip area is dominated by the high–data-rate systems.

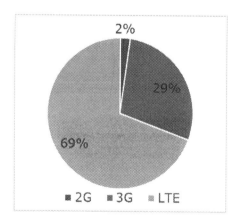

Figure 2-2. *Implementation complexity (= chip area) dominated by 3G and LTE*

However, when we normalize this area to the data rate, the comparison is inverted: The low–data-rate systems have a higher complexity per received bit than the high–data-rate systems, as shown in Figure 2-3.

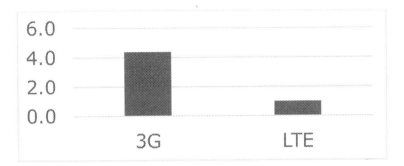

Figure 2-3. *Increasing receiver performance of mature air interfaces: area normalized to data rate*

While the air interfaces are definitely different and cannot be compared so simply, it is still a fact that over time, as air interfaces mature, more advanced receivers will be integrated into the modem. Those advanced receivers are usually missing in early generations. Through more stringent performance requirements by standardization and by experience gained in the field in real-life deployments, interference cancellation or mitigation techniques are introduced, and baseline receivers get closer to maximum-likelihood performance, as shown in Figure 2-3. Overall complexity is still dominated by the air interface that has the highest data rate.

Radio Frequency

While Moore's Law helps scaling all digital parts nicely, it affects the analog parts of a cellular system differently. The difference starts with the number of bands a UE has to support for worldwide coverage. 2G allows global coverage with four bands (850 MHz, 900 MHz, 1800 MHz, and 1900 MHz, corresponding to LTE bands 5, 8, 3, 2). 3G (WCDMA) also allows coverage with four bands: bands 1 (2100 MHz) and 8 (900 MHz) give good coverage outside America, where bands 2 (1900 MHz) and 5 (850 MHz) are needed. To support specific regions and operators, further 3G bands may be added. As of today, many chipsets now support five WCDMA bands.

However, with LTE and its new Carrier Aggregation (CA) feature, the situation is getting confusing. As of March 2016, there are roughly 50 LTE bands specified. Chipsets supporting around 30 bands are common. Furthermore, as specified by the 3GPP RAN4 working group, there are almost 600 CA combinations of up to five carriers in four bands specified so far, with new combinations being added at an accelerated rate. Right now, standardization activities are under way to support signaling of up to 32 carriers for CA (3GPP Release 13). Because most of the CA combinations are operator-driven, it's likely that many will actually be deployed.

Network Infrastructure

In order to anticipate the transition toward 5G network infrastructure, let us first consider the previous transition from 3G to 4G networks.

Evolution of the Network Architecture

The 3G radio access network (RAN) architecture consisted of multiple nodes in a hierarchical fashion, namely the base station (called NodeB or NB in 3G jargon), providing the radio connection, and the Radio Network Controller (RNC), which supervises multiple NBs, typically within a specific area. Subsequently, the RNC is connected to the core network, which connects to all the numerous services, from voice to data, in the operator network and the Internet.

4G provided a radically different approach, flattening the architecture and reducing the number of nodes in the RAN to a single node only, the base station, now called enhanced NodeB (eNB) to differentiate it from its 3G counterpart. This approach made the RNC redundant. The functionality that was formerly contained in the RNC, in particular affecting the management of the air interface directly, was integrated into the eNB, including the aspects we will discuss next.

Scheduling

Frequency domain scheduling gain provided a significant contribution to the performance advancements brought by 4G. Because any latency adversely affects the scheduling gains achievable, scheduling was advanced to the eNB, eliminating any delay from going back and forth over the backhaul link between NB and RNC. Strictly speaking, a first transition toward this principle was already initiated in 3G when High Speed Downlink Packet Access (HSDPA) was introduced; this also contains fast scheduling performed by the NB (albeit only in the time domain, not yet in the frequency domain). However, because 3G still had to support legacy Release 99 services, a hybrid architecture had to be maintained, in which both RNC and NB implement similar functionalities for legacy circuit-switched services as for packet services introduced later. By fully relying on packet services and emulating legacy circuit-switched services, 4G finally eliminated this redundancy. Another reason for sacrificing the RNC was that *soft handover* was no longer required. It was essential to allow operation of WCDMA with frequency reuse one; that is, reusing the same resource from multiple NBs and sending/receiving concurrently to/from the multiple NBs. As short-term fluctuations may make the connection to one or the other NB better over the time, using both links simultaneously ensures that the best link is always available to carry the communication. From the user equipment (UE) point of view this is almost transparent; it is not much different from receiving a signal containing two echoes due to reflections.

The second "reflection" is actually an individual transmission, but all that is needed from the UE perspective is to apply the parameters used by the second NB for this path. Otherwise, processing via a rake receiver can commence as usual. On the network side, however, soft handover involves a significant complexity increase, as data from multiple NBs relating to the same UE need to be collected at a central node (that is, at the RNC) in order to pick the best received copy (indicated by a checksum, for example) of the data, frame by frame. Even better, all received signals are forwarded from all involved NBs to the combining node, and the received data is inferred, thereby taking all information from all received raw data into account (this is called softer handover). To make this possible, these (raw) data need to be forwarded via backhaul links toward the central node, more than doubling the load on the backhaul links.

Without soft handover, there is no need for a central node above the NB to determine the data; instead, it is done in the eNB. The performance gain obtained by soft handover isn't required for 4G anymore, because scheduling gain is available in both the frequency and time domains and can be utilized on a much faster timescale, of 1 ms. This gain is sufficient to maintain the communication even if the link toward the serving eNB suddenly becomes worse than toward neighboring cells, at least until a handover to the better cell has been performed.

Interference Mitigation

Ironically, the lack of the RNC, while it was welcome in the initial version of the standard, came to be seen as a disadvantage in later versions of LTE, starting with LTE-Advanced, as the RNC might have been a suitable place to coordinate the behavior of multiple eNBs to optimize interference coordination. The section "Evolution of Inter-Cell Interference Mitigation Schemes in 4G Systems" later in this chapter describes these ICIC techniques from the UE perspective. The UE certainly appreciates them as being "interference mitigation techniques relying on smart networks, which are able to adjust the scheduling in such a way that cell edge users experience a reduced level of interference." While this takes away all the burden from the UE, to the delight of UE vendors, the network is burdened with determining the suitable parameters for all the schedulers' behaviors. This cannot be decided locally at each eNB, because it depends on all the neighboring eNBs as well; they must mutually agree which resources to use exclusively in one eNB for that eNB's cell edge UEs and which resources to keep free in adjacent eNBs. Of course, it would be easy to set aside sufficient resources at each cell edge in a static approach, but if a particular cell edge is not populated by many UEs, this approach is highly inefficient as the reserved resource would sit idle in adjacent cells for no advantage. Therefore, an advanced network implementation will communicate the need for cell edge resources to be protected from neighbor cell interference among neighboring eNBs and have them agree on the specific resource allocation to select under the currently experienced network load distribution. This communication can be done peer to peer between adjacent eNBs over the so called X2 interface, which was standardized to exchange the relevant information.

Self-Organizing Networks

In addition to this decentralized approach, further functionality was subsequently introduced via enhancements in a centralized way. For example, in the framework of Self-Organizing (or Optimizing) Networks (SON), a higher hierarchical element was reintroduced into the network hierarchy, similar to the RNC. It should be noted, however, that this element does not affect the data path that carries the bulk of the user data; it is used only for configuration purposes, to configure all involved nodes, links, and procedures optimally given current network conditions. As such, it does not cause additional latency in the data path, because the data does not traverse it. Similarly, an overload situation in any SON entity does not cause an immediate degradation of user services, as these don't touch any of the SON entities. Only the continuous network optimization may be interrupted for some time, but if the network situation doesn't change dramatically in the meantime, that shouldn't affect the performance.

To summarize, 4G networks made it possible to clean up the 3G network hierarchy after it had grown exuberantly over the course of 3G's deployment and introduced a much more streamlined, simpler, and more efficient approach. As subsequent LTE releases have brought more enhancements, 4G has itself seen many additions, requiring new paradigms that have had to be somehow retrofitted to the existing network. Soon, it will again be time to introduce a new architecture that supports all recently integrated functionalities and optimizations in a consistent way. 5G networks offer the opportunity to establish such new paradigms, supporting all the features we know from 4G and many more in a seamlessly integrated, holistic way.

Network Nodes

While the network architecture is a decisive aspect of a system, in the end the network is built from individual nodes. The complexities, costs, and deployment constraints of these nodes determine the total network cost and ease of deployment. The actual implementation in hardware (HW) also needs to be considered. Moore's Law, as presented earlier, of course predicts advancements in the network infrastructure and allows deployment of compact, high-performant nodes, but there are further aspects to consider.

First, because spectrum is limited, a major share of capacity enhancement needs to be achieved by site densification (see the section "Spectrum Management Vectors" in Chapter 4, "5G Technologies"). This necessitates the rollout of more and more cells, partly in the form of higher sectorization, but eventually also by deploying more and more base stations. This involves several challenges for the network operators:

- Acquisition of multiple base station sites

- Rollout of the initial deployment

- Configuration of all these base stations

- Optimizing parameters to reduce mutual interference

- Connection of all sites to the backbone at low cost

- Upgrades and enhancements when traffic increases

Traditionally, base stations came in the form of 19-inch racks, filled with multiple radio frequency (RF) units, digital baseband (BB) processing units, and auxiliary units for things like cooling, power supply, backhaul connection, and maintenance functions. Because of their sheer size, these racks require a dedicated space for deployment, such as a hut at the base of an antenna tower in outdoor deployments or a dedicated room within a building for rooftop deployments. Thanks to technology advancements, these huge racks can now be shrunk to small boxes that can be bolted to walls or hung at antenna posts easily without much preparatory installation or need for civil engineering at the sites. By reducing site requirements, the number of feasible sites increases and consequently site acquisition gets less difficult.

Small and easy-to-deploy eNB form factors ease network rollout, but this has to be augmented by an automatic configuration of freshly deployed nodes. Otherwise, the administrative effort would eventually become prohibitive as the number of nodes increases. This automation is achieved by SON functionality, which allows eNBs to detect their environment and connect to neighbor eNBs for agreeing on proper resource utilization across eNBs (*see Chapter 4, "5G Technologies," for a discussion of context-aware networking and SON evolution*).

The backhaul link, connecting an eNB to the gateway, is a significant cost driver in particular if new cables have to be laid or lines have to be leased. An alternative for backhaul is microwave, already used extensively for base stations. 5G will introduce the option to use microwave links for communications to the UE (see Chapter 6, "The Disruptor: The Millimeter Wave Spectrum"). This will also offer the opportunity to leverage the same technology for both access and backhaul. This corresponds to the Type 1 relay introduced in LTE-Advanced [2]. However, the latter was rather restricted, as it had to be retroactively introduced into the LTE Release 8 framework, using MBSFN subframes, requiring deviations from the existing channels. Usage of relays onboard vehicles, such as high-speed trains, was also restricted, as LTE does not allow changing fundamental cell parameters on the fly. As a consequence, some parameters may cause clashes with existing eNBs along the route. For 5G it will become essential to have the system versatile to seamlessly support access and backhaul for both fixed and mobile nodes from the beginning without unnecessary constraints or complexity (*see Chapter 4 sections "Wireless Backhauling" and "Opportunistic/Moving Networks"*).

Adapting networks to keep pace with ever-growing traffic demand is an ongoing operator effort. Aside from densification, that is, introducing additional base stations, this can also be achieved by upgrading existing base stations to support more channels, users, or data and to introduce advanced processing and scheduling capabilities for higher efficiency. For 19-inch racks this typically involved slotting in additional hardware such as advanced BB processing cards, or swapping old cards with more powerful new ones. However, as the number of nodes increases, the "all nodes" approach becomes more cumbersome and costly. A more comfortable way to increase BB capabilities recently emerged in the form of CRAN (Cloud RAN), in which the base stations deployed in the field primarily contain RF functionality (so-called remote radio heads), and the BB processing for many base stations is concentrated at a central site. Now BB upgrades for multiple sites can be done comfortably at a single site. Furthermore, processing resources can be liberally shared among base stations dynamically in response to spatially varying traffic patterns. 5G needs to ensure that network virtualization concepts can be easily deployed (*see "Networking and Virtualization Approaches" in Chapter 4*).

Future Evolution

A significant legacy aspect of 4G is that the UE was allowed to make assumptions about the signals (in particular pilot signals) received from the eNB, which limits the freedom of network implementation and evolution. This dilemma trades off network flexibility against UE implementation complexity, not only for the implementation effort but also the UE's validation and testing. Because 5G will need to work for a decade at least, and will evolve further based on evolving requirements, it needs to be future-proof itself and not already be overly constrained in its first release.

LTE, on the other hand, was possibly too rigidly defined initially, in particular in the distribution of crucial resources, like the cell-specific resource symbols (CRS), that don't allow any variations. Fortunately, LTE in the end still has some whitespace in the form of the Multicast Broadcast Single Frequency Network (MBSFN) subframe. Intended to provide broadcast and multicast services, it was not finalized in time for the first release; instead a placeholder was provided that was intended to be filled with the final MBSFN subframe definition in the next release. By then it had already become apparent that this unintentional "white space" could actually be used not only for the intended MBSFN support but also for various functionalities, including relaying (imperfectly, as stated earlier) and heterogeneous network support.

In 5G it will be essential to come to a reasonable compromise that neither burdens the UE too much nor restricts network evolution. The target is to achieve a future-proof system that can easily evolve and respond to subsequent requirements. Already the first definition of 5G needs to be done with a forward-looking mindset and should contain sufficient "white spaces" that are not immediately defined but deliberately set aside to be later used to support new concepts.

Operational Challenges

Current and future 4G networks have to overcome several big challenges:

- How to manage highly diverse deployment strategies and topologies?

- How to maintain a consistent user experience across all network layers and locations in interference-rich environments?

- How to reduce cost per bit to maximize the return on investment?

Meeting End-to-End Quality of Service (QoS) in 4G networks has been a key operational challenge from the beginning. Challenges include varying data rates and bandwidths, highly diverse channel characteristics and interference, handovers in heterogeneous layouts, and high fault-tolerance levels. During the development of LTE a special focus has been packet-level QoS such as throughput, latency, packet error rate, and handover delays.

Within the evolution of LTE to LTE Advanced, theoretical peak data rates increased from 300 Mbps in the downlink direction and 75 Mbps in uplink (Release 8) to 3 Gbps in the downlink and 1.5 Gbps in the uplink (Release 10). The most important feature LTE-Advanced introduced to meet those requirements was carrier aggregation (CA). Current devices use up to three component carriers (CCs) in downlink and two CCs in uplink with up to 450 Mbps and 100 Mbps. Furthermore, 3GPP specifies MIMO extensions up to 8×8 in the downlink direction and 4×4 in uplink. Additional uplink access enhancements have been introduced to enable those requirements, including clustered SC-FDMA, simultaneous data and control information (PUSCH and PUCCH transmission), improved cell edge performance (enhanced inter-cell interference coordination (eICIC), and relaying.

LTE-Advanced Pro maximum downlink and uplink data rates are expected to exceed 3 Gbps and 1.5 Gbps, respectively. This can only be achieved by combining at least 100-200 MHz carrier aggregation in downlink with 4 × 4 MIMO and 256 QAM. Some of the carriers might be in an unlicensed band. In uplink, 50-100 MHz carrier aggregation, 2 × 2 MIMO and 64 QAM can be combined to deliver data rates exceeding 1 Gbps. Obviously, such enormous data rates put a high burden on network and terminal operations in terms of complexity, scalability, and power consumption.

Packet data latency is one of the performance metrics used by network vendors, operators, and end-users to measure end-to-end QoS as it not only shows responsiveness of the system but also impacts overall system throughput and buffer requirements; that is, longer RTTs require larger data buffers. There are many existing applications that would benefit from reduced latency by improving perceived quality of experience, such as gaming, real-time applications like VoLTE or OTT VoIP, and video telephony or video conferencing. Furthermore, the number of delay-critical applications will increase: we will see remote control and autonomous driving of vehicles, augmented reality applications in smart glasses, and specific machine communications requiring low latency as well as highly reliable communications [3].

Various prescheduling strategies can be used to lower the latency somewhat, but like the shorter Scheduling Request (SR) interval introduced in Release 9, they do not necessarily address all efficiency aspects. Reduced latency of user plane data may indirectly reduce call set-up/bearer setup times thanks to faster transport of control signaling. To improve the packet data latencies, 3GPP introduced a study item on latency reduction [3]. The basic principle is to shorten the TTI to the first seven OFDM symbols, that is, the first slot (0.5 ms). The 3GPP recommendation is to maintain the control region of the subframe without modifications and ensure a minimum number of OFDM symbols for the physical channels in the data region. The study will include resource efficiency, air interface capacity, battery lifetime, control channel resources, specification impact, and technical feasibility.

Reduced latency brings, however, new issues and constraints in UE designs. UEs need to remain backward compatible with the existing LTE UEs, that is, new design should preserve the same OFDM symbol duration, CP durations, tone spacing, operations in all possible symbols (CRS, control region) and should follow existing LTE procedures [4]. Backward compatibility is especially important in TDD mode, where several cycles are required for delivering one scheduled round trip transmission of control or data signaling. Additionally, the total air interference latency is limited by its physical frame structure, that is, by the minimum enabled UL/DL switching time [5]. Therefore, new UEs will require flexible and fast link-direction switching and short guard times between the link directions. Different lengths of TTI will result in different amounts of over-the-air latency reduction, different performance, and reduced coverage (at UL). Thus, the new UEs might be designed with configurable TTI lengths. Also, more dynamic demodulation reference signals (DMRS) design at UL and faster channel state information (CSI) feedback will be required to handle uplink overhead and processing [4].

Higher data rates and shorter latencies have the additional benefit of reducing handover delay when moving from the coverage area of the serving cell into the coverage area of a neighbor cell, as the required signaling (measurement reports) can be transferred in shorter time. For instance, in 3G systems, a measurement report can take up to 120 ms. In LTE, this is reduced to only a few ms.

Interference Issues in 4G Networks

In most cases, 4G networks are deployed as single-frequency networks; that is, frequency reuse is 1. This might be the most efficient in terms of spectrum, but by nature single-frequency networks are limited by inter-cell interference. As 4G network deployments are diffusing and network traffic is increasing, along with a huge diversity of applications, LTE-Advanced and LTE-Advanced Pro network deployments are trending to heterogeneous layouts using small cells. Those networks are capable of handling demanding coverage and capacity requirements, particularly in hot-spot areas that generate the highest traffic volume. Additionally, in those deployments cells can be dynamically switched on and off to increase energy efficiency. However, in such heterogeneous deployments, interference becomes highly exacerbated and comes from diverse sources.

Network-Based Interference Management

The LTE and LTE-Advanced standards have already provided a toolbox to mitigate interference, comprising techniques like MIMO, beamforming, and scheduling. After Release 10 introduced eICIC (enhanced inter-cell interference coordination) in 3GPP, Releases 11 and 12 introduced feICIC (further enhanced ICIC) leveraging new transmission modes and schemes such as CoMP (Coordinated Multipoint Transmission). The concept of Almost Blank Subframes (ABS) was introduced to coordinate data transmission from macro and micro cells in heterogeneous deployments; the subframes are blanked except for the signals needed for legacy operations (like reference or synchronization signals). The signaling needed to coordinate a decision between several base stations has been defined to support both reactive and proactive X2-based inter-cell interference coordination schemes, which is being fully exploited in early LTE network deployments. Inter-cell interference mitigation techniques are explained in more detail in the section "Evolution of Inter-Cell Interference Mitigation Schemes in 4G Systems."

Terminal-Based Interference Management

A significant drawback of network-based interference solutions is that they limit capacity efficiency and increase signaling overhead. Thus, smarter receiver algorithms are gaining interest as another potential driver for significant improvements in network performance. This was anticipated by 3GPP and led to the standardization of interference-aware receivers for UMTS and to similar concepts for LTE receivers. Terminal-based interference mitigation concepts have the following user and operational benefits:

- Overall throughput increase

- Improved QoS and coverage across the entire cell

- Improved performance and throughput for cell-edge users

- Improved service continuity across the network

Table 2-1 gives an overview of LTE-Advanced receivers up to today.

Table 2-1. *LTE-Advanced Receivers*

3GPP Release	Receiver	Network Layout	Interference Source	Network Assistance
Release 11	MMSE-IRC	Homogenous	PDSCH	no
	CRS-IC	Heterogeneous	CRS	yes
Release 12	NAIC	all	PDSCH, CRS	yes
	SU-MIMO IS/IC	N/A	Intra-cell PDSCH	N/A
Release 13	CRS-IC	Homogenous	CRS	yes
	MU-MIMO IS/IC	all	Intra-cell PDSCH	TBD
	Control IM	all	PDSCH, CRFS, (E)PDCCH	CRS
	MMSE/IRC for 4RX	Homogenous	PDSCH	N/A

In summary, there are three key types of receivers applied in LTE Advanced networks for interference suppression, cancellation, and mitigation (IS/IC/IM):

- MMSE-IRC (interference rejection combining (IRC) according to the minimum mean squared error (MMSE) criterion) leverages the interference correlation across multiple receiver antennas and adds a spatial interference whitening filter in front of the standard MMSE receiver.

- CRS-IC (interference cancellation of cell-specific reference signals (CRS)) explicitly cancels CRS interference of neighbor cells. Applicability is usually restricted to synchronous networks.

- NAICS (network assisted interference cancellation and suppression) adds signaling of interferer characteristics, like modulation schemes.

In general, IS/IC/IM techniques can be applied to all kind of signals based on explicit cancellation, but it usually requires a high effort, and there are much simpler scaling techniques. Proper link adaptation mechanisms by adjusting the rank or channel quality indication feedback signaling can support all those techniques.

Receiver Design under Resource Limitations

The telecommunications industry faces the challenge that the spectral resource is becoming scarcer and scarcer. As discussed in the previous sections, because of the limited spectrum, most 4G networks are single-frequency deployments. In this context, one of the lessons learned from 4G technology is that spectrum usage efficiency can still be improved, in particular with respect to out-of-band and spurious emissions characteristics. In order to enforce this objective, the European Commission has revised the Radio Equipment and Telecommunications Terminal Equipment (R&TTE) Directive of 1999 [6], which defines the basic requirements to be met by all radio equipment in the single European market. The R&TTE Directive will finally expire in 2017 and be fully replaced by the new Radio Equipment Directive (RED) [7]. The RED contains substantial changes related to spectrum usage efficiency:

Radio Equipment and Telecommunications Terminal Equipment (R&TTE) Directive - Article 3: Essential requirements [6]: "*In addition, radio equipment shall be so constructed that it **effectively uses the spectrum allocated to terrestrial/space radio communication and orbital resources** so as to avoid harmful interference*";

Radio Equipment Directive (RED) - Article 3: Essential requirements [7]: "*Radio equipment shall be so constructed that it **both effectively uses and supports the efficient use of radio spectrum** in order to avoid harmful interference*".

It is obvious that the new wording will put pressure on future standardization and equipment manufacturing activities to have an improved and interference-free coexistence between systems operating in neighboring spectra. In order to drive the modified requirements efficiently in standards bodies, CEPT's Spectrum Engineering (SE) Working Group [8] is currently working toward the definition of a new methodology for coexistence studies. The objective is to finally reduce guard bands between systems that are located next to each other in frequency domain. This objective can, for example, be met by reconsidering more precise models for characterizing spurious emissions in digital systems. A corresponding report is entitled "Review of receiver parameter and receiver behavior to achieve a more efficient use of the spectrum" and available at the Working Group site [8]. To give a specific example, it was observed through measurements that state-of-the-art digital systems often operate considerably below the spurious emissions limits except for harmonic frequencies. If such observations are taken into account for coexistence studies performed by regulation administrations, a more efficient usage of the spectrum will become possible.

A further substantial change in the transition from the R&TTE Directive [6] to the RED [7] is that regulation administration will mandate the provision of receiver parameters in the applicable Harmonized Standards. In the past, standards mainly focused on transmission parameters with the intention to leave receiver design to equipment manufacturers; still, some receiver parameters were already included in relevant standards at least for some systems. It has been understood in recent years, however, that the lack of receiver specifications negatively impacts the efficient usage of the spectrum. To give an example, implementing spectrum sharing is challenging if no information is available about the receiver sensitivities of incumbent systems. This issue will be resolved in the future by regulation administrations mandating an explicit definition of receiver parameters in applicable Harmonized Standards. On the other hand, this trend may impact the competitive landscape since the performance of equipment provided by various manufacturers will finally meet identical requirements.

Interference Mitigation Features in 4G

To use the available resources optimally, LTE is designed with a frequency reuse of 1, allowing operators to use their available radio frequency spectrum efficiently. On the other hand, having radio transmissions on the same frequency in two neighboring cells is bound to create interference, degrading the overall system capacity and creating a user perception of throughput problems and call drops. Therefore, operators are strongly interested in developing and deploying methods that limit or even avoid heavy inter-cell interference.

Evolution of Inter-Cell Interference Mitigation Schemes in 4G Systems

The first interference mitigation feature that was foreseen in the Release 8 standard was inter-cell interference coordination (ICIC). With ICIC the network uses the power and frequency domains to mitigate cell edge interference from neighboring cells. For example, the network may assign different sets of resource blocks to cell edge users belonging to different eNBs, while for users in the center the full resource block without restriction can be utilized. This way, the cell-edge SINR for the traffic channel is significantly improved without sacrificing the major part of the cell throughput. ICIC was developed for homogeneous macro networks without small cells placed inside the macro coverage. Information is shared between neighboring eNBs via the X2 interface.

In Release 10, ICIC was evolved to eICIC to better handle DL interference in heterogeneous networks where ICIC cannot be applied, because the small cell is located entirely inside the macro coverage. In addition to the power and frequency domains, eICIC also includes the time domain for interference coordination, which works by dividing all subframes into almost blank (ABS) and non-ABS subframes. Macro and small cells are able to operate in a time-division multiplex manner where the macro cell schedules only its terminals in non-ABS subframes, while the small cell exclusively uses the ABS subframes for DL data. ABS subframes contain only the bare minimum physical channels to ensure support of legacy terminals, such as the synchronization channels (PSS/SSS), the physical broadcast channel (PBCH), and the paging channel, SIB1, as well as the cell specific reference signals (CRS); they also create less interference than non-ABS subframes. In addition, ABS subframes can often be transmitted with less power than non-ABS subframes. Whether a subframe is ABS or non-ABS is communicated via RRC signaling as a semi-static pattern to the terminal. To allow the network to select the ABS pattern according to the current load and interference levels seen by the terminals, those terminals provide separate CSI information for the two sets (ABS and non-ABS) to the network.

In Release 11, eICIC has further evolved to feICIC, addressing the interference created by channels still present in ABS subframes, that is, synchronization channels (PSS and SSS), PBCH, and CRS. Interference from the synchronization and broadcast channels renders cell search a challenging task, particularly in synchronous networks where interfering synchronization sequences overlap with the synchronization sequences of the serving cell. To this end, 3GPP has specified demodulation requirements for these channels based on successive interference cancellation mechanisms. Particularly in scenarios with a high cell range expansion, up to 9dB the CRS interference can degrade PDSCH (Physical Downlink Shared Channel) performance considerably. Thus, techniques to mitigate this interference (colliding and non-colliding) must be employed to meet the performance requirements expected by the operators.

eICIC and feICIC were developed for HetNet scenarios where traffic is offloaded from the macro cell toward small cells (any of which could be a pico cell, femto cell, or even a remote radio head) and are based on the assumption that a sufficient number of small cells is placed in the macro area, allowing the introduction of ABS subframes that are not used for DL data by the macro cell. Thus, for heavily loaded macro networks a sufficient number of small cells have to be placed such that the throughput gain coming from the small cells compensates for the throughput loss due to the introduction of the ABS subframes. Even with this assumption, the problem of inter-cell interference at the cell edge between two macro cells is not fully addressed, as introducing ABS subframes in homogeneous macro networks is only affordable in lightly loaded cells.

Another interference mitigation method that does not rely on ABS patterns is cross-carrier scheduling (CCS), introduced in Release 10 along with carrier aggregation (CA). With CCS it is possible for the network to map the downlink control channel (containing the downlink control information (DCI)) and the DL payload to different DL carriers. If applied in a HetNet scenario the network may map the DCI of the macro and the small cell to different component carriers. Similarly, in a macro-macro interference scenario, the network may separate the DCI of both macro cells by mapping them onto different component carriers, thereby reducing DL control channel interference for cell edge users. To broadly apply this technique, it is of course mandatory that the majority of the UEs support Release 10 CA along with cross carrier scheduling. For high end terminals this prerequisite is usually met, as CA is a method of boosting the data rate. On the other hand, pressure to keep prices low for low-end terminals usually requires the chip manufacturer not to provide support for CA, thus excluding cross-carrier scheduling as a viable option for this class of terminals.

Network Assisted Interference Cancellation

The interference mitigation techniques introduced earlier, such as ABS, CCS, and so on, predominantly rely on smart networks, which are able to adjust the scheduling in such a way that cell edge users experience a reduced level of interference. A different class of DL interference mitigation techniques relies on more complex receiver algorithms, thereby avoiding scheduling restrictions imposed by the network; such restrictions alone may reduce system capacity.

The first feature belonging to this new class was introduced in Release 12 and is called Network Assisted Interference Cancellation (NAICS). In NAICS mode the terminal is able to remove PDSCH interference prior to demodulation of the serving cell PDSCH. Usually this is done either by implementing a successive interference cancellation receiver, which estimates the interfering PDSCH and subtracts it before it is demodulated, or by employing a joint detector, which demodulates serving and interference PDSCH jointly. To support NAICS the network signals semistatic parameters to the terminal, while estimation of dynamically changing parameters is done in the terminal blindly. Despite network support, NAICS increases terminal complexity significantly as all parameters required to demodulate an interfering PDSCH, such as channel estimation, the precoder, the modulation type, and so on, must be estimated in real time in parallel to the parameters required for the serving cell.

While NAICS improves demodulation performance for the PDSCH channel, Release 13 introduces the feature Control Channel Interference Cancellation (Control Channel IC), which aids in reliably receiving the PDCCH, PCFICH, and PHICH channels carrying the downlink control information. The specification sets forth tighter demodulation requirements, using improved receiver algorithms that make use of channel estimates of an interfering PDCCH/PCFICH/PHICH channel. While this is the first improvement in demodulation performance for the DL control channels from the 3GPP side, most chipset manufacturers have already implemented some sort of enhancement for the control channels in order to stay ahead of the competition.

Further improvements in performance for the DL data and control channels are expected through the cancellation of CRS interference, a feature that is standardized in Release 13 and is called CRS-IC.

Figure 2-4 compares implementation complexity in terms of MIPS/gates as well as control complexity (1= Low, 2.5 = medium, and 5= high) on the UE side to demodulate a serving cell PDSCH channel in the presence of interference as a function of the interference related features standardized by 3GPP since Release 8. In the remainder of this section we refer to the complexity in terms of MIPS/gates as the processing complexity.

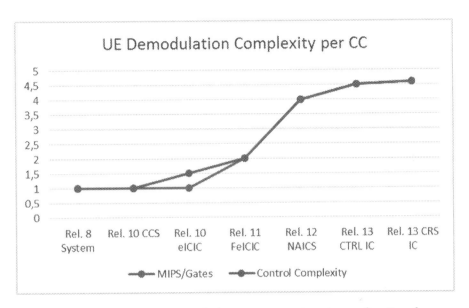

Figure 2-4. *UE implementation complexity per component carrier as a function of interference-related 3GPP features*

Assuming an implementation complexity of 1 for a Release 8-compliant system (where the network applies ICIC to handle inter-cell interference), it can be seen that the Release 10 features eICIC and cross carrier scheduling (CCS) increase the control complexity by 50%; this is mainly to handle the two subframe sets that have to be taken into account during computation of the CSI feedback. The processing complexity, however, is not increased.

A major step in control and processing complexity must be taken with the introduction of feICIC, which requires the UE to explicitly take into account the channel estimation of interfering CRSes by either subtracting them with the right interference power level, or by explicitly considering this interference in the computation of what are called *whitening filters*. Compared to a Release 8 system this step is significant, and so we quantify it with a factor of 2.

The next major increase in both control and processing complexity is the introduction of NAICS in Release 12. The reason for the increased complexity is quite simple, as under NAICS, channel estimation must be carried out for an interfering PDSCH; in terms of processing complexity this is much more involved than feICIC, where only interfering CRSes are considered. Both CNTRL-IC and CRS-IC further increase control as well as processing complexity, but this increase is not as significant as the introduction of NAICS.

The numbers illustrated in Figure 2-4 provide only very rough guidelines and are intended to help visualizing the major drivers on the UE side. It is clear to the authors that the numbers themselves are arguable, and to come up with a more solid complexity analysis, all of these features need to be looked at in much more detail.

Performance Optimization and Productization

Productization - The act of modifying something to make it suitable as a commercial product. Productization is a conceptual stage not to be confused with production [10].

Optimizing a cellular system in the field requires us to consider many impacts (Figure 2-5). Of course, the chipset needs to be optimized in terms of power consumption and modem performance. Beyond the chipset, the phone design has an impact, obviously (for example, via the antenna design, which is constrained by the form of the device), but also less obviously via configuration options of certain applications. The cellular network itself plays a central role, where dependencies on data plans or time of day (such as rush hours and weekends) are seen. Overall, on the terminal side as well as on the network side, certain features need to be enabled on both ends to achieve their benefits.

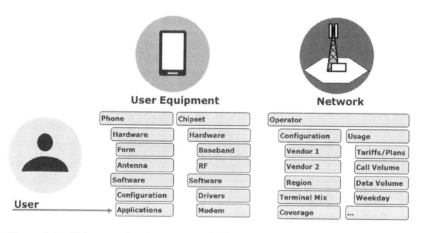

Figure 2-5. *Chipset productization: a multidimensional challenge*

Once a mobile device is used in the field, a couple of years of specification and development work have already passed. Assuming that the lifetime of a certain mobile platform is two years, with a planning and development time of another two years, the specification of a mobile platform needs to anticipate markets and requirements for at least those future four years (Figure 2-6).

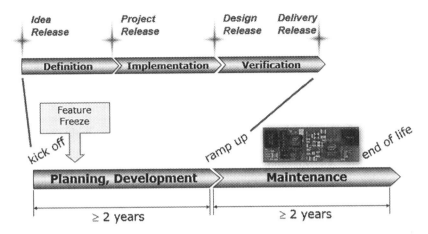

Figure 2-6. *Lifetime of a mobile platform*

Depending on the required level of detail, this goal can easily become impossible: apps usually have much shorter innovation cycles; network deployments can change over time, reacting to user demand; and interference scenarios might change accordingly. Hence, it is required that a cellular platform has sufficient flexibility to react to potential change requests with robust upgrade mechanisms, usually via firmware updates.

As shown in Figure 2-7, the basic phases of product development consist of the following:

1. *Definition*: The product idea is selected from the roadmap to develop the customer and market requirements. Basic features are defined, technical feasibility and risks are assessed, features are translated into product requirements, and receiver algorithms and the basic hardware architecture are specified.

2. *Implementation*: The product is developed from a concept into a product design. The product is subsequently partitioned into components, subcomponents, and basic modules. Verification objectives of the respective hierarchical levels are specified. Hardware and software are coded. The final hardware design is handed over to a silicon factory, and software needs to be feature-complete.

3. *Verification*: The product needs to be integrated and verified. The silicon is manufactured and the individual modules and components are stepwise brought up. After bring-up is complete, it needs to be proven that all specifications and requirements are met and that the product is ready for mass manufacturing, that is, for the first production version to be released. This verification phase is highlighted in a bit more detail in the following section, "Test Efforts."

4. *Maintenance*: Finally, after the product is ready to be delivered to customers, manufacturing continues to be optimized, as well as the performance in the field.

Figure 2-7. Product development phases

Test Efforts

The verification phase of launching a mobile phone platform begins with a couple of distinct stages, starting with a first simple stationary call against a system tester with a default configuration. This is followed by a basic call against a live network (if available).

The next level of maturity is reached by achieving conformance with certification bodies like GCF (The Global Certification Forum) or PTCRB (PCS Type Certification Review Board). This ensures 3GPP compliance of the cellular platform. Typically a few thousand conformance test cases are required for 2G, 3G, LTE, and 2G/3G/LTE interworking. Because the 3GPP standard allows a vast number of possible configurations, this 3GPP compliance does not necessarily guarantee that a specific platform also works properly in a live network.

Hence, interoperability testing (IOT) with network equipment vendors and operators is required for live network operation in a specific network. The number of inter-operability test cases is typically a few hundred per company. Once all operator approvals are in place, a product can be launched in the field.

As the field reality spans a vast range of conditions, including untested and unexpected interference or radio propagation environments, a final optimization in the field is required. This includes testing on predefined routes and regions, and also random testing.

Figure 2-8 illustrates the related maturity levels. You can see that the maturity level is increasing by an order of magnitude from step to step. It is important not to confuse the maturity level with importance, as all test phases are equally important.

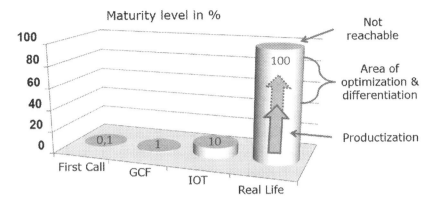

Figure 2-8. *Maturity levels*

Figure 2-9 illustrates the overall platform development efforts. As you can see, roughly half of the effort is spent after the first bring-up is done and roughly a quarter of the overall effort is spent after the first production version is released, emphasizing the importance of the final productization in the field.

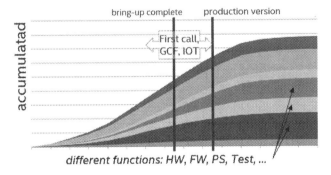

Figure 2-9. *Platform development efforts*

Aspects Affecting End-to-End User Experience

The GCF, IOT, and operator tests can consider by design often only very specific scenarios. A certain test case usually checks only one specific aspect. However, in real life many different aspects are relevant for the end-to-end user experience, and many of these aspects contradict each other. Thus, these test cases may not in the end be very relevant for a product that is well received by the end user.

For example, considering only single mobile devices, there is a conflict between the improvement in demodulation performance brought by advanced receivers with features like diversity reception and interference cancellation, and the consequently increased power consumption, which reduces the battery lifetime. The performance gain by the advanced receivers is checked by certain test cases, but the additional power consumption is not measured or considered.

When we consider the mobile device behavior in a complete network with many other devices, other conflicts arise: for example, the mobile device transmits at high power as long as possible before a connection loss, but this high transmit power causes interference for other users and the overall network. Thus, there are test cases that require the mobile device to shut off the transmitter very early when going out-of-sync. The end user would instead prefer to keep the transmitter on as long as possible, to avoid the connection drop. Thus, the algorithm design has to find a balance between these aspects.

The following sections provide some further aspect and examples, highlighting the difference between certification lab tests and the real life.

Link Adaptation

Link adaptation (LA) has been included since the first full LTE release (Release 8). The basic idea of LA is that the terminal provides information about its current DL channel conditions to the network, which can then adapt its scheduling in the DL accordingly. For example, if the channel conditions degrade, the network can reduce the coding rate, change the modulation order, or switch from a two-layer transmission back to a single layer transmission to reach a desirable point of operation in terms of block error rates (BLER) with a reasonable receiver complexity.

Figure 2-10 shows the basic relationship between complexity on the receiver side and throughput.

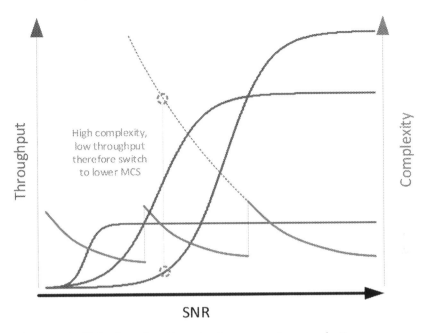

Figure 2-10. *Link adaptation: throughput versus receiver complexity*

For high SNR, the higher the modulation and coding scheme (MCS), the higher is the achievable throughput. As mentioned earlier, this higher throughput is achieved by using a higher modulation order, that is, for instance, 64 QAM instead of QPSK, by increasing the number of streams, or by increasing the coding rate. As long as the SNR is high enough, any MCS can be decoded at the receiver side with reasonably low complexity. However, as the SNR decreases, decoding of a high MCS requires increasingly complex receiver algorithms, for example, a sphere decoder instead of an MMSE detector, or advanced joint channel/coding algorithms, leading eventually to an undesirable operating point. In order to limit the necessary receiver complexity, the network may reduce the MCS values for the DL as the SNR goes down. At very low SNR, only very robust modulation schemes like QPSK, a single layer, and a very robust coding scheme are used, allowing the receiver to decode the transmitted data bits with reasonable decoding complexity. In summary, link adaptation is a mechanism used to strike a balance between high throughput for high SNR and low receiver complexity at low SNR.

LTE link adaptation (LA) is based on measurement information that the terminals provide to the network: the channel quality indicator (CQI), the precoding matrix indicator/precoding type indicator (PMI/PTI), and the rank indicator (RI). Depending on the reporting mode, CQI and PMI can be signaled as wideband values, which are then interpreted by the network as best values if applied to the entire bandwidth, or as subband specific values, valid only in a specific range of the complete system bandwidth. Depending on the transmission mode the terminal reports one CQI value for both code words, or one CQI value per code word. The rank indicator informs the network on the number of spatial layers the terminal is able to receive under its current channel conditions. The network on the other hand is free to use or not use the received information for the selection of the DL MCS transmitted to the terminals.

While the general idea and concept of LA is simple, providing close to optimal CSI information to the network is nontrivial. According to 3GPP, calibration of the terminal and its CSI reporting should be done in such a way that the block error rate for initial transmissions is 10 percent or less. If the LA is too aggressive the BLER goes up, resulting in a throughput loss due to decoding errors on the terminal side. On the other hand, a too conservative LA may cause the network to use transport formats with a code rate lower than necessary, also resulting in throughput loss. To achieve optimal throughput a well-calibrated link adaptation is therefore mandatory.

What makes implementation difficult is the large number of parameters in an LTE system: ten transmission modes, four periodic reporting modes, and six aperiodic reporting modes. Beyond the parameters of the LTE system itself, there are at least six 3GPP channel types that need to be considered, varying from low to high delay spread, and from static to 300 Hz Doppler channels in addition to a myriad of real-life channels. The result of this large parameter space is a high control complexity, usually also leading to an increase in the required memory as all of these different modes must be handled slightly differently.

Another important factor to consider is that verification of the chipsets is done using several types of test equipment, such as Callbox testing and testing with real infrastructure hardware.

Callbox testing: Here the terminal is usually connected directly to the callbox via a rather ideal cable, and the callbox generates a channel model based on the selected parameters, such as Doppler bandwidth, delay spread, and so on. The callbox usually follows the reported terminal metrics, such as CQI, PMI, RI, directly without processing them. The received CSI information is directly mapped into suitable DL parameters, such as MCS format and is transmitted on the DL with the correct timing. For example, CQI values are mapped more or less directly into MCS values without filtering them and without checking whether the applied values provide performance close to the target BLER or not. Hence, when doing performance comparisons between two implementations based on callbox testing, it is very important to have a well-calibrated device that behaves well for SNR sweep tests under different fading profiles. CSI calibration errors are very visible in these kind of tests.

Infrastructure testing: When carrying out infrastructure tests, the terminal is also connected via cables to the eNB as in callbox testing. However, in contrast to a callbox the eNB usually applies some kind of outer loop link adaptation (OLLA) to the received CSI information before mapping it into a DCI transmitted to the terminal to achieve a certain target BLER. Besides this, the processed CSI metrics affect not only the selected DCI in the DL, but also the scheduling rate of the UE. In particular, infrastructure tests with multiple terminals providing sub-optimal CSI metrics may lead to scheduling the desired terminal at a low rate and, for example, an interfering terminal at a high rate. Calibration errors are usually not so visible in infrastructure tests, due to OLLA. On the other hand, optimal performance in infrastructure tests can only be achieved if the behavior of the eNB is known to the terminal. For example, does the eNB follow the rank decision of the terminal directly, or does the eNB apply filtering algorithms to the received CQI metrics? To make things complex, different network vendors treat and process the CSI metrics in different ways, but one chipset has to work optimally, or close to optimally, in all networks.

Over the air (OTA) testing: In OTA tests the network equipment and the terminal are usually placed in an anechoic chamber where it is possible to carry out cable-less tests in a controlled way.

Field testing: The ultimate test: LA has to assume that certain parameters are set in a certain way and computes the CSI metric accordingly. Since a UE does not know what the eNB does with the metrics, it is difficult for the UE to decide whether eNB is following or not.

Sometimes a UE does certain things that are not specified in the standard. For example, with CQI filtering, the CQI should normally reflect the situation of one specific subframe. With some kinds of filtering, throughput can be improved in certain networks.

One more challenge is to tune the CSI in such a way that it works optimally with all eNB equipment manufacturers and also well with callbox testing.

Call Drops

Dropped calls belong to the most annoying experiences of end users. Figure 2-11 illustrates a real life example in which an incomplete neighbor cell list, combined with a specific local topography, causes frequent call drops. The call drops frequently happen when the mobile platform moves along the red path on the large main roadway, which is lowered for quite a stretch at an underpass of another road. At the beginning the serving cell is cell A, which has cell B but not cell C in its neighbors list. The network planning assumes a handover to cell B, which has cell C in its neighbor cell list. Because of the high buildings and the lowered roadway, however, cell B is usually not strong enough to trigger a handover to it. When the lowered roadway ends and the signal from cell A becomes very weak, there is the good cell C available. However, because cell C is not in cell A's neighbor cell list, the mobile platform needs to do a complete search of all cells to detect cell C. This frequently results in a call drop.

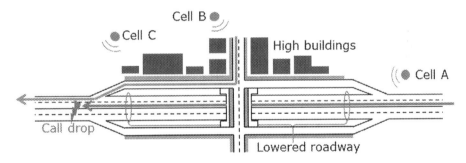

Figure 2-11. *Call drop due to incomplete neighbor cell list*

Interestingly, the likelihood of the call drop also depends on the speed of the mobile platform on different parts of the red path, varying for example due to traffic. A higher traffic speed means a faster degradation of the signal of cell A. But it also means the mobile device arrives earlier in the zone covered by cell C; that is, it has a longer time to acquire that signal. A stop caused by a traffic jam at the right position near the underpass could also allow the device to get cell B as its serving cell.

Some further points to note in this case are also valid in many other scenarios. For example, the root cause for the call drop happens quite some time before the actual call drop. If cell A had indicated cell C as a neighbor cell when cell A became a serving cell, the call drop would not have happened. The importance of the history is also obvious when we consider the green route. Devices taking the green route experience no call drops at the place where frequent call drops occur along the red route, because on the green path, cell B indicates cell C as one of its neighbor cells and the mobile platform can detect it easily with this knowledge. Local topography also plays an important role. The lower roadway and high buildings block the cell B signal and are essential for the frequent call drops on the red route.

Throughput

Throughput—that is, the achievable data rate—is a critical key performance indicator in today's and future wireless networks. It is measured in various ways. One aspect is the peak data rate defined by a particular standard, which at least partly reflects the network capacity of the network operator for a cell and also serves marketing purposes. Another aspect is the effective throughput seen by the end user in a personal use case; we will examine some considerations for that shortly.

Field versus Lab Testing

Lab testing for conformance and performance is usually executed *conducted*, that is, the devices are connected by a cable to the test equipment. This approach allows for precise settings, but many effects of live network environments are not considered. The example in Figure 2-12 shows that the results of conducted throughput benchmarking tests with different form-factor devices from multiple vendors are typically very close together; that is, all devices perform within a tolerance of 1 dB in SNR. Independent benchmarking publications also suggest that "the industry may need to move away from conformance-based testing as defined by 3GPP" [9].

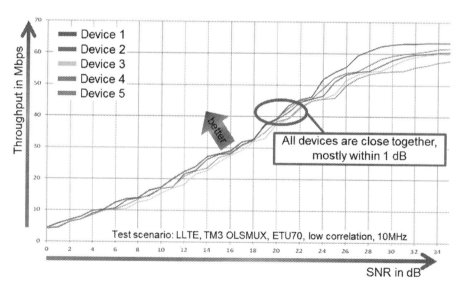

Figure 2-12. *Conducted LTE throughput benchmarking lab test*

A first step toward bringing more real world parameters into the lab is over-the-air (OTA) *radiated* testing in the lab. Here, the device is no longer connected by a cable to the test equipment. Instead, in an anechoic chamber a controlled test radio environment is created. This allows the antennas of the test devices to be considered, for example in terms of their radiation patterns. Throughput tests now often show performance deltas of up to 10 dB for a single device, depending on its rotation position, front or back, to the main RF signal sources. This demonstrates the limited relevance of conducted lab test results for real-world performance in a live network, which is what's relevant for the end user, in terms of usability of his device, as well as for the operator, in terms of the network capacity overall. Still, OTA testing in the lab still neglects many influencing parameters seen in the field.

The following examples demonstrate some of these effects seen in field testing in the real world. Figure 2-13 shows the results of a simple throughput test experiment in a live LTE network. Two identical tablets are placed next to each other, about 5 cm apart. Then, 40 iterations of throughput testing are done, where each iteration consists of an FTP download of a 50 MB file from the same server, with the download started on both devices at the same time. After 20 iterations only the positions of the devices are swapped.

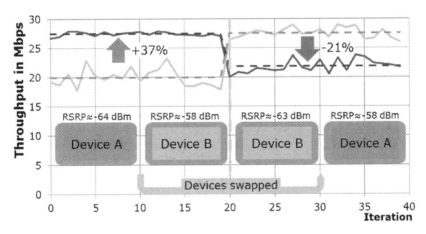

Figure 2-13. *Throughput test with two tablets next to each other*

While the blue device A before the swap consistently exhibits a significantly higher throughput than the green device B, the situation is reversed after the swap, when device B has the higher throughput. Evaluating the signal strength in RSRP of the devices reveals that at the left position the received signal strength is approximately 6dB, that is, better by a factor of 4, despite the positions being only a few centimeters apart.

This signal strength dependency becomes especially critical for uplink throughput. When the mobile platform has a large amount of data to upload, it will transmit at its maximum transmit power to maximize the uplink throughput. With this limited transmit power the throughput then depends almost solely on the transmit power actually radiated by the antenna in the direction of the base station and the path loss between mobile platform and base station. For example, a delta of 3 dB in path loss usually implies a factor of 2 in uplink throughput, with a delta of 1dB already yielding a factor of 1.25. With less path loss, the same maximum transmit power is sufficient to have more resource blocks transmitted by the mobile platform, reaching the base station at the desired SNR.

With downlink throughput in LTE reaching levels far beyond 100 Mbps—for example, LTE CAT6 offers 300 Mbps and CAT9 450 Mbps—the wireless link between mobile platform and base station is no longer the only part that is challenged by the high data rates; other parts also become critical. For example, on the network side, the source of the data, such as the FTP server, as well as the Internet and the core network of the cellular network must all be able to provide these high data rates to the base station for all its users. And on the mobile platform side, the bus system from the modem to the application processor of the device must sustain these data rates, and the application processor must also be able to handle and process the huge amount of data.

Neighbor Cell Measurements and Handovers

As in the call drop example described earlier, neighbor cell measurements and handovers play a critical role for the throughput observed by the end user, especially in mobility scenarios. Figure 2-14 illustrates some key parameters for throughput during a handover based on an example from a live network test. The figure is a simplified sketch of real data taken from a similar test like the one shown in Figure 2-13, where we see two devices doing a parallel data download, but with the added factor of mobility.

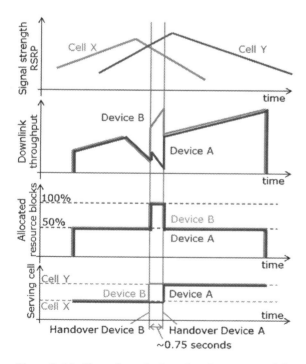

Figure 2-14. *Throughput during a handover in a mobility test*

Before the handover, both devices are on cell X, with the pink marked RSRP measurements. It can be further observed that the two devices each get about half of the possible network resources; that is, resource blocks. This means the two devices seem to be the only (or main) users in this cell.

During the mobility test, cell Y (with the RSRP shown in brown) becomes the best cell. At this point the throughput starts dropping because of the interfering signal of cell Y. Eventually, the two test devices make a handover to this cell Y. However, because of different neighbor cell measurement strategies and slightly different reception conditions, as described in [9], the two devices do the handover about 0.75 seconds apart, with the blue device A being the later one. It can be seen that in the short phase after green device B has done the handover to cell Y and device A has not, device A gets all the resources from cell X, which should result in high throughput. But because cell X is worse than cell Y, the throughput of device A stays low, and only jumps up when device A also does the handover to cell Y. Here, the device B with its earlier handover to the better cell Y had the better strategy. Thus, this example shows that a handover to the right cell at the right time is critical to achieving good throughput performance.

Roll-out of New Features in Existing Networks

Even though new features are standardized, their roll-out in live networks generates challenges and requires a certain time for adaptation and maturing the feature. Both the mobile platform and the base station may encounter unforeseen obstacles, for example in the standard or in an early release of the equipment, for which the main target was time-to-market.

Figure 2-15 visualizes an example of immature base station behavior, which has been observed in multiple networks at the launch of LTE CA. With the enabling of CA, a significant increase in throughput is expected. In the example scenario both carrier had a bandwidth of 20 MHz. Thus, approximately a doubling of the throughput was anticipated.

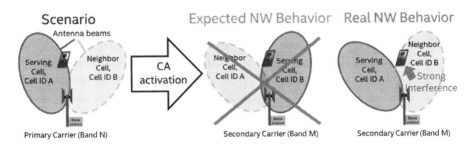

Figure 2-15. *Example of live network obstacle for LTE carrier aggregation*

The throughput measurement was done at a location where, on the primary carrier on band 7, the serving cell for the mobile platform had cell ID A. There was a neighbor cell with cell ID B visible in the measurements, but the signal-to-noise ratio for the serving cell was still very good. Yet, on the secondary carrier, which was on band 20, the RF environment was different. The operator use similar cell IDs on both carriers, which simplifies network planning. However, because of aspects like slightly different positions, tilts, or rotation of the base station antennas, or different propagation conditions of high band 7 and low band 20, the cell with cell ID B was the best cell for the mobile platform. Thus, the expectation was that cell ID B is the serving cell on the second carrier. Unfortunately, the network had the limitation that the serving cell IDs of the primary and secondary carrier had to be identical, probably to anticipate the network planning mentioned earlier. This caused, at the use measurement location, strong interference on the second carrier, because the weak cell A was the serving cell in the presence of the strong cell B. As a consequence, there was no relevant increase in throughput when CA was enabled, contrary to expectations.

This example shows that in early live deployments of features, obstacles are often encountered in certain scenarios, even if the features are standardized.

References

1. Moore, Gordon E. (1965-04-19). "Cramming more components onto integrated circuits" *Electronics*. Retrieved 2011-08-22.
2. Holma, H., Raaf, B., & Redana, S. "Relays. LTE-Advanced: 3GPP Solution for IMT-Advanced," pp. 110–134, Wiley, August 2012, ISBN: 978-1-119-97405-5.
3. 3GPP RP-150309, "Study on Latency reduction techniques for LTE," 3GPP TSG RAN WG1#67, March 2015
4. 3GPP R1-157082, "On physical layer aspects of low latency operation" 3GPP TSG RAN WG1#83, Nov. 2015
5. E. Lähetkangas, K. Pajukoski, J. Vihriälä, G. Berardinelli, M. Lauridsen, E. Tiirola, P. Mogensen, "Achieving low latency and energy consumption by 5G TDD mode optimization," IEEE ICC2014, June 10-14, Sydney, Australia
6. DIRECTIVE 1999/5/EC OF THE EUROPEAN PARLIAMENT AND OF THE COUNCIL of 9 March 1999 on radio equipment and telecommunications terminal equipment and the mutual recognition of their conformity, Official Journal L 091, 07/04/1999 P. 0010–0028.
7. DIRECTIVE 2014/53/EU OF THE EUROPEAN PARLIAMENT AND OF THE COUNCIL of 16 April 2014 on the harmonization of the laws of the Member States relating to the making available on the market of radio equipment and repealing Directive 1999/5/EC, http://data.europa.eu/eli/dir/2014/53/oj.
8. CEPT Spectrum Engineering, http://www.cept.org/ecc/groups/ecc/wg-se
9. Signals Ahead, "Chips and Salsa XIX: LTE-Advanced Carrier Aggregation Chipset Benchmark Study", Signals Research Group, Vol. 12, No.3, February 2015
10. https://en.wiktionary.org/wiki/productization

CHAPTER 3

Evolving from 4G to 5G

As discussed in the previous chapters, the definition of each cellular standard has been driven by a set of key use cases.

Their evolution was driven by market requirements. Building on analog technology, 1G was designed for voice only. The step to digitization was achieved in the context of its evolution to 2G, offering improved voice and text messaging. 3G was designed to support integrated voice as well as low-cost and low-data mobile Internet. The current cellular system, 4G, represents a substantial redesign of legacy technology to provide high capacity and data for massive mobile services. Future 5G technology (Figure 3-1) is expected to build on a combination of existing and new, revolutionary technologies designed to meet extreme capacity and user demands. It will need to enable connectivity for a wide range of applications with high social and economic values. 5G will lead us into an "all-time connectivity society" where mobile devices will play an even more important role in people's lives. 5G will be not only a cellular standard but a combination of cellular and other heterogeneous standards. In this chapter we will focus on the cellular characteristics of 5G.

Main Drivers for 5G

5G will be driven by completely new services and requirements. It is expected that there will be billions of connected objects by 2020 [1] and data rates of several Gb/s, supporting the individual user experience at low latency and response time. As shown in Figure 3-2, it is expected that the first commercial deployments of 5G will be built in the run-up to the Tokyo Olympics in 2020, and its development will further evolve until 2030.

© Intel Corp. 2016
B. Badic et al., *Rolling Out 5G*, DOI 10.1007/978-1-4842-1506-7_3

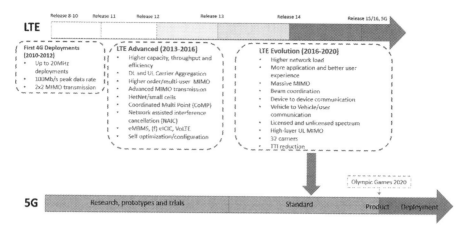

Figure 3-1. *LTE's evolution toward 5G*

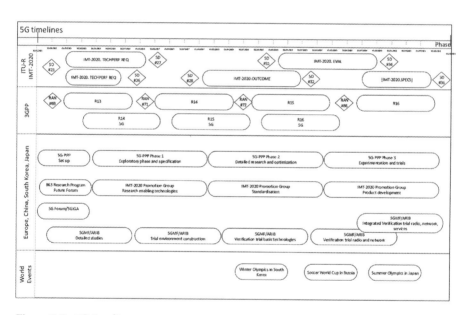

Figure 3-2. *5G timelines*

The content and the number of applications will dramatically increase in the next years. Enhanced camera resolution, 3D imaging, and increased screen resolution are only a few factors driving the completely new requirement sets for 5G. Always-on connectivity and push services for applications like streaming services, interactive video, and games have to be guaranteed.

The dramatic number of new use cases and the inherent requirement for devices with different form factors present challenges for the entire industrial landscape. While a small number of major smartphone manufacturers currently supply the market with state-of-the-art mobile devices, 5G is expected to shift productization to a large number of smaller players for addressing specific niche markets. It is foreseen that those industries will build on development kits and open source access to tailor their respective products to selected markets. Naturally, major players will supply commercial mass markets.

The current LTE standard cannot meet all of those demands. For example, during the 2012 Olympic Games, the mobile network became jammed by the heavy mobile traffic, which prevented organizers from receiving important information on timing and position. The problems reported at the Olympics indicated that the current network infrastructure is not keeping up with the growth in demand for it. Even though network providers started preparations several years before 2012, the mobile network was not ready for such a high volume of consumers using mobile to engage in social media, watching and sharing videos, and otherwise consuming content via mobile networks.

Huge public events offering the opportunity to spotlight national capabilities are driving the time schedule. Ericsson expects to showcase some 5G-based scenarios during the winter Olympics in 2018 [3]. South Korea, the host of the 2018 Olympics, is investing $1.5 billion into a 5G network [4]. NTT DoCoMo revealed plans to roll out 5G commercially for the 2020 summer Olympics [5]. The company expects to deliver 5G through a variety of massive MIMO (Multiple-Input-Multiple-Output) and 128 polarization elements within the antenna arrays, along with narrowbeam transmission to each user. It is expected that NTT DoCoMo's total throughput delivered will be in excess of 25 Tbps.

Definition and Use Cases for 5G

Usually, when work begins on defining a new system, certain key use cases are identified that need to be supported in an optimized manner and will provide novel functionalities beyond the capabilities of legacy technology. As discussed in previous chapters, for 2G this was voice, and then 3G was designed to support Web browsing in addition to voice, first in Release 99 and from Release 5 on with *High Speed Packet Access (HSPA)*. But although there was hype about video telephony, it never reached the mass-market. LTE was a natural extension of HSPA to allow higher throughput.

It should be noted, however, that many popular use cases arose during the operation of those systems that were not anticipated during the specification phase: SMS was unexpectedly one of the main revenue sources for 2G operators; the introduction of smartphones and social networking together with Fast Dormancy brought many 3G networks close to collapse; and LTE development started in 2005—before the introduction of smartphones. Hence, use case discussions about 5G will have some aspect of the crystal ball.

Even though it is generally acknowledged that 5G will be the next cellular standard, it is still not described or defined in any particular specification or any official document published by an official telecommunication standardization body. 3GPP has started work on 5G technologies and defined a 5G timeline [5], however it does not explicitly use the term "5G" [5].

Representing major mobile network operators, Next Generation Mobile Networks (NGMN) has published a white paper on 5G [6]. The definition of 5G given there is more a prediction of future mobile networks beyond 2020 than a specific vision of the underlying technologies that will enable 5G. However, it is clear that 5G will introduce completely new and revolutionary concepts. Those technologies and solutions are currently being discussed among network operators, semiconductor manufacturers, standardization bodies, and research institutions. Therefore, the definition of 5G use cases, requirements, and enabling technologies will extend over several years.

It is expected that 5G will be unlike previous generations. The major differences will not be merely combinations of old and new radio access technologies; *5G will also enable new use cases and requirements* of mobile communication beyond 4G systems. It will be an integration of existing cellular standards and technologies, including new disruptive technologies like mmWave and spectrum sharing.

The evolution of LTE in Release 14 is expected to offer a first step toward 5G by enabling wireless access for frequency bands below 6 GHz. Hence, LTE Advanced Pro might be considered a special case of 5G in those frequency bands. For higher bands, a new *radio-access technology (RAT)* and inherent supporting and integration solutions will be introduced. Therefore, the 5G architecture will be an integration of *Multi-RAT*, supporting the simultaneous operation of multiple heterogeneous technologies. Next to mobile broadband radio access, 5G will incorporate systems that enable *massive machine-type communications* (MTC). Within Release 13, 3GPP already specifies NB-IoT (Narrowband Internet of Things) to operate within a 200 kHz bandwidth. In the work on 5G specifications, this is expected to be further optimized toward a high number of supported devices, low device cost, and ultra-low power consumption.

To provide the required capacity and features, 5G will build on the following three main pillars, as illustrated in Figure 3-3:

- *More spectrum*: Access to a new spectrum in the upper mmWave bands and new spectrum usage paradigms such as spectrum sharing

- *More spectrum efficiency*: Not necessarily in terms of link capacity as described in Shannon's Theorem, but through better exploitation of the entire heterogeneous environment

- *denser deployment*: To be enabled by the use of small cells

Figure 3-3. *Pillars enabling 5G*

While all three of the pillars in Figure 3-3 are essential parts of 5G, a specific challenge is the provision of additional spectrum. In traditional wireless systems, carrier frequencies up to about 6 GHz have proven to be suitable for mobile usage. Unfortunately, this part of the spectrum is fully allocated to a variety of incumbents, and opportunities for repurposing spectrum to commercial cellular usage are becoming scarce. To address this challenge, regulation administrations and standardization bodies such as ETSI in its RRS (Reconfigurable Radio Systems) Technical Committee and 3GPP have recently developed spectrum-sharing solutions, which allow secondary usage of cellular applications while incumbents leave the band unused in a specific geographic area and during a specific time period. In Europe, the technology is called Licensed Shared Access (LSA) and addresses sharing in the 2.3-2.4 GHz band. In the US, an even more innovative approach has been introduced, called Spectrum Access System (SAS), targeting the 3.55-3.7 GHz band. In both cases, a key challenge lies in a system definition that enables a viable business model. This requires all of the following: long-term investment certainty (guaranteeing access to spectrum on a multiple-year basis through suitable sharing agreements), and guaranteed QoS, and exclusive access to spectrum (during the absence of incumbent users, the access needs to be prioritized for the cellular Mobile Network Operators (MNO) under a suitable sharing agreement), and protection of confidential information (avoiding any public sharing of detailed configuration information by spectrum licensees).

In parallel to spectrum-sharing technology, a further complementary technology is being developed. In cmWave and mmWave bands above approximately 10 GHz, available frequency bands can still be identified and allocated to commercial cellular usage. However, the viability of corresponding technology for various use cases (static indoor, nomadic, pedestrian, high speed, and so on) is currently under study [15] and needs to prove its suitability. The outcome of this evaluation obviously impacts the (potential) need for sharing technologies below 6 GHz dramatically. Key challenges to be studied and addressed are the increased propagation losses at higher frequency ranges, the need for 3-dimensional propagation models to take specific multi-antenna patterns into account, system behavior in the context of user and environment mobility, and the suitable configuration of highly directional transmissions.

As illustrated in Figure 3-3, the second pillar in the three-pillar model relates to an increase in spectral efficiency. Although link-level capacity purely on a physical layer and for a given available bandwith is unlikely to see a substantial increase in efficiency, the potential resides in layer two (Medium Access Control) and higher layers. Indeed, the amount of overhead (signaling, management, and so on) in recent wireless communication systems has reached an intolerable level. More intelligent management of overhead, possibly in a cross-layer approach, is a key direction to be studied in future 5G systems. Furthermore, it is obvious that in cellular modem architecture, new design breakthroughs and changes are necessary to meet these 5G goals. A solution with feasible implementation complexity including resource sharing across different RATs of individual building blocks like working memory and data path logic will be needed. Figure 3-4 shows an example. Naturally, the cellular modem architecture explained in Chapter 2 will undergo significant changes at the system and component level.

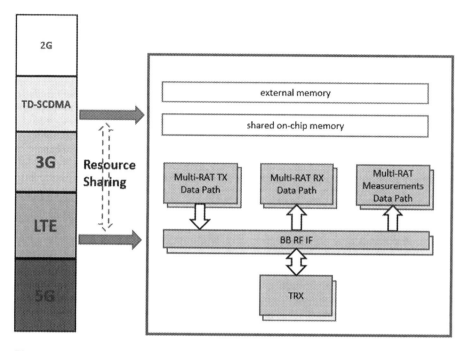

Figure 3-4. *5G Multi-RAT architecture*

Finally, the third pillar in the model shown in Figure 3-3 relates to densification. The benefits of moving from macro base stations to densely deployed small-cell setups are twofold: First, the smaller coverage area provided by a small-cell compared to a macro base-station typically means a smaller number of users, assuming that the distribution over space is comparable. Consequently, the available resources can be distributed across a reduced number of users and thus more capacity is allocated per user. Second, thanks to the denser deployment of small cells, users are typically closer to the base-station antenna, and thus the signal propagation conditions are more favorable. Indeed, propagation losses and similar effects are reduced, and thus a more spectrally efficient transmission mode (such as denser modulation constellations, a less redundant channel code, and so on) can be employed. In consequence, the observed QoS of concerned users is substantially improved.

It is important to note that the three pillars are mutually independent. Consequently, the observed effects are multiplicative. For achieving targeted capacity gains in the order of 1000 to 10,000 times, as it is typically requested for 5G systems over 4G technology, a straightforward way is to assign a factor of $\sqrt[3]{1000} = 10 \dots \sqrt[3]{1000} \approx 22$ to each of the pillars in Figure 3-3. The final choice may deviate from this initial guess, but these numbers give a good first idea of the engineering challenges for 5G.

Research and Development Ventures

New services and corresponding requirements to be provided to mobile users beyond 2020 are already driving the vision of 5G use cases. Many companies and market analysts have published white papers on 5G applications and use cases [6]-[12]. As shown in Figure 3-1 earlier, the race toward 5G started years ago, coming into full swing by kicking off private and public efforts in 2015. Whereas the governments in China and South Korea have been aggressive in setting up national 5G research and development projects, the European Union perches on public-private partnerships, and the United States relies more upon private companies.

European and Asian governments have been particularly active in driving 5G. In China the activities are coordinated by the National Development and Reform Commission (NDRC), the Ministry of Industry and Information Technology (MIIT), and the Ministry of Science and Technology (MOST), converging into the IMT-2020(5G) Promotion Group. Likewise, the European Commission has launched the 5G Infrastructure Public-Private Partnership (5G-PPP) to deliver what will be the ubiquitous 5G communication infrastructures of the next decade, including solutions, architectures, technologies, and standards. In Japan, companies like NTT DoCoMo, in partnership with companies like Ericsson, Fujitsu, NEC, Nokia and Samsung, are contributing to the "2020 and beyond" group established by Japan's Association of Radio Industries and Businesses (ARIB). South Korea has established the 5G Forum, driven by its Ministry of Science, ICT, and Future Planning. In the United States, academics and private enterprises are deeply involved in 5G-related research and development. For example, the NYU Wireless program of New York University's Polytechnic School of Engineering is researching technology deemed crucial to 5G, including millimeter-wave. And as another example, Verizon has been working with Cisco, Ericsson, Intel, Nokia, Qualcomm and Samsung to start 5G field trials at its Waltham and San Francisco Innovation Centers in 2016.

Based on those activities, a set of 5G goals has been identified that are not linked to specific use cases but rather describe how 5G networks should be built and what they should deliver:

- 5G should be designed to support *billions of connected devices and users* across the globe and support a *diverse set of services and applications.*

- 5G will be required to deliver *1,000 to 10,000 times higher cell capacities and user data rates* than its predecessors.

- 5G will need to deliver *low latencies* in order to avoid the bottleneck of radio interface and to guarantee real-time reliable connections with an exceptional user experience.

- *High coverage and availability* will be two strong business cases of 5G. Difficult and specific geographic areas should be covered by a 5G network.

- 5G should be built in a scalable and flexible way in order to deliver *high energy efficiency* and as such *prolong battery life*. For example, 5G will only transmit and receive when needed.

- Despite the simultaneous usage of a multitude of heterogeneous RATs, *maximum output power levels and aggregate power* budgets need to be achieved.

- Typical *form factors* of 4G devices will need to be maintained for mass market 5G applications. Furthermore, a plethora of niche market application will require specific tailored form factors and inherent software adaptations (typically enabled through open source).

- Existing 2G, 3G, and 4G systems are expected to be kept operational in the mid- to long-term, that is, for the next 10 years and beyond. 5G-capable devices thus need to provide *backward capability* for specific use cases (for example, 2G may continue to provide low-cost, low-data-rate services, 3G/4G technology may be used in locations where 5G is not yet rolled out, and so on).

- 5G systems will have access to further frequency bands within the classical frequency range *below 6 GHz* as well as in the cmWave and mmWave spectrum *above 10 GHz*. Multiple bands across multiple frequency ranges will be combined and operated simultaneously through advanced, possibly heterogeneous Carrier Aggregation (CA) schemes, which still need to be defined.

Use Cases

5G will have to provide solutions for a broad range of devices, operating in a fully heterogeneous environment. As illustrated in Figure 3-5, these use cases and applications are new and more complex than ever, and the major challenge in 5G design will be how to support such heterogeneous use cases in a scalable and reliable way.

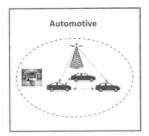

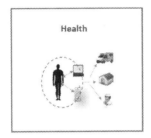

Figure 3-5. *5G use cases*

Mobile broadband access and service availability are key use cases driving the requirements for 5G. This family of use cases covers broadband access everywhere, including densely populated areas and challenging areas in terms of coverage, consistent user experience and service availability for new services such as streaming (audio, 3D video), interactive video, mobile Internet connectivity (high-mobility connectivity), and operator cloud services.

The *automotive* future will create many use cases enabling mobile communication in vehicles. Content-related use cases such as passenger entertainment and reality dashboards will require simultaneous high mobility broadband and capacity. On the other hand, use cases related to car safety include driver assistance systems, as well as communication and information exchange between vehicles and other connected devices; these use cases will become a challenge in 5G systems as they require high reliability and low latency.

The Internet of Things (IoT) is a family of use cases covering massive number of devices such as low-cost and low-power MTC or human type communication (HTC) devices.

It is expected that most of those devices will be connected within a 5G network. Therefore, 5G will result in a *smart society* with use cases such as smart cities, smart homes, smart offices, and smart grids. Those use cases will require high bandwith and fast completions of complex applications, which in turn will require high-speed processing of a large amount of data.

With 5G it is expected that *health-related* applications will continue to grow and new ones will emerge. Lifeline fitness and healthcare-related applications and services will require ultra-reliable, prioritized, and reserved system capacity, both inside and outside of network coverage with security and privacy ensured for each user.

Extreme real-time communications is a family of use cases that will impose a high demand in terms of *real-time interaction* [6]. Tactile Internet, remote computing, and autonomous driving are among the applications that will need to rely upon robust mobile links and high availability.

Because 5G is expected to support a substantially higher number of users than 3G/4G with high capacity and at the same to keep latency and cost low, the optimization of use cases will obviously be complex and multidimensional. For a comprehensive description of use cases please refer to [6].

Requirements

The use cases just discussed are leading to diverse and extreme requirements. NGMN has published a document defining and specifying the first set of 5G requirements and KPIs according to the respective Use Case Categories [6], with a set of requirements representative of an extreme use case in that category (Figure 3-5). It is expected that not all requirements will be fulfilled for the launch of 5G in 2020; they will be the subject of further discussion among operators and vendors involved in defining 5G. As was the case for 1G to 4G, a stepwise extension of the feature set is likely to be defined and introduced to the market.

Evolving 4G Features to Support 5G Use Cases

Because 4G is the fastest-growing cellular technology, mobile operators will continue investing in its development until at least 2020. Based on the GSMA report [7], it is expected that mobile operators will invest $1.7 trillion in network infrastructure through 2020, and much of this will be in 4G networks.

At the same time, 3GPP continues to develop 4G standards, as shown back in Figure 3-1. The LTE Release 12 specification, frozen in September 2014, is built on LTE-Advanced. The majority of Release 12 requirements are already related to some of the 5G goals, such as an enormous traffic and capacity increase, energy and cost efficiency, and support for advanced applications and services, all coupled with higher user data rates.

Following are the key LTE enhancements specified in Release 12:

- Small cells and heterogeneous networks (dual-connectivity (DC), higher-order modulation)

- Multi-antennas enhancements, such as MIMO and beamforming

- Network Assisted Interference Cancellation (NAIC)

- Proximity services, ProSe (Device to Device Communication)

- Procedures for supporting diverse traffic types

- Machines Type Communication (MTC)

Release 13 introduced further enhancements for NAIC, ProSe, DC and CA for up to 32 carriers. Active Antenna Systems (AAS) and SON for AAS-based deployments, elevation beamforming, a procedure for latency reduction, Licensed Assisted Access (LAA), and

Inter-eNB CoMP (Coordinated Multi-Point) have also been introduced as further features. A comprehensive summary of Release 12 and Release 13 can be found in [13].

LTE Evolution (LTE-Advanced Pro)

Release 14 will be a release in which a first set of 5G features will be defined (IMT-2020). Together with Release 15, it will serve as a building block for 5G under the (draft) brand LTE-Advanced Pro. The Specification of LTE-Advanced Pro will be driven by the following technical requirements:

- Improved spectral efficiency

- High traffic density

- Massive connectivity

- Lean design

- Support for cmWave and mmWave transmissions

- Integration of LTE and 5G RAT

To fulfill those requirements, new features together with enhanced features from previous releases will be discussed and specified during the Release 14/15 timeline. Figure 3-6 illustrates key components and characteristics of Release 14 and their relationship to 5G requirements.

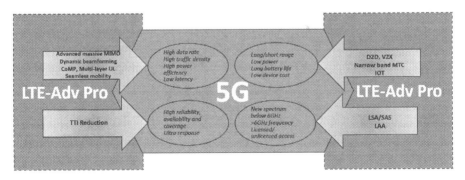

Figure 3-6. *LTE-Advanced Pro features and 5G requirements*

Massive MIMO, multilayer UL (Uplink) MIMO, and CoMP will be enhanced to improve spectral efficiency, capacity, user-experienced data rate, and mobility. Improving beam coordination and introducing over 16 antenna ports will lead to increased data rate and improved interference mitigation. Flexible beam-cell operation will allow seamless mobility, fast transmission points, and beamswitching and minimization of RRC signaling. With seamless mobility, almost zero service interruption time will be achieved by minimal configurations at network and UE.

The initial studies on Release 12 showed that device-to-device communication, (D2D), also known as proximity services (ProSe) communication, has advantages such as increased spectral efficiency and reduced latency, but it introduces serious challenges in terms of implementation, complexity, and interference to cellular networks. Release 14 will introduce new enhancements in D2D design to support ultra-dense, multi-layer, and interference-rich networks. It is also expected that D2D communication will become an intrinsic part of the IoT and vehicle-to-vehicle/vehicle-to-pedestrian communication (V2X), where D2D will be used to pass any information from the vehicle to any entity that might affect the vehicle and vice versa. Standalone devices or devices built in vehicles will autonomously communicate with each other, without requiring any central node control. They will collaborate, gather, share, and forward information in an ad-hoc way. Road safety, traffic management, and in-car entertainment will be improved. In the longer term for 5G, V2X will enhance assisted and autonomous driving.

One of the key 5G requirements, latency reduction, will be an important element of Release 14. The primary focus will be to reduce existing TTI (Transmission Time Interval) to the first slot (the first 7 OFDM symbols) for any transmission. Reduction of TTI will have some implications in control channel and reference symbol (RS) design.

A particular focus of Release 14 will be spectrum utilization. Further enhancements of LAA to support an UL LBT (Listen-Before Talk) procedure and multiple carriers will be studied. LSA/SAS support in the U.S. 3.5 GHz band will be also studied.

3GPP plans 5G trials in 2018; these will be based on Release 14 study items and initial Release 15 working items. Furthermore, initial 5G commercial deployments are expected to be based on the Release 15 specification. The IMT-2020 submission will be based on Release 16 specifications.

A Closer Comparison of 5G and 4G

Figure 3-7 summarizes the vision of 5G networks, showing its key differences from 4G and where the two cellular standards will intersect. In summary, 5G networks will do the following:

- Deploy a *multitude of heterogeneous RATs* where mobile devices may operate multiple links to distinct RATs simultaneously

- Deploy a *multitude of different cell types,* including dynamic cell structuring mechanisms

- Combine classical wireless broadband bands, typically below 6 GHz, with *mmWave* bands

- support the application of *wireless backhauling,* in particular for small cells

- Deploy *several base stations* to serve a target mobile device simultaneously

- Enable *device-to-device and multi-hop* communication

- Enable usage of an *efficient User/Control plane split* across multiple BS and/or multiple RATs

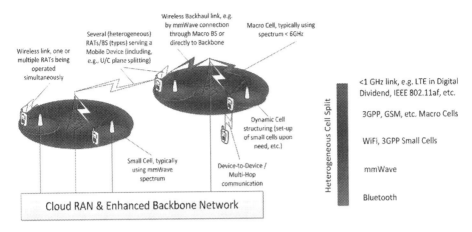

Figure 3-7. *A 5G network and its key features [14]*

The 4G air interface is based on OFDM waveforms, which provide system bandwidth scalability, multi-user resource allocation in time and frequency, with a granularity of physical resource blocks (PRB = 1 ms × 180 kHz), and spatial MIMO processing at moderate signal processing complexity. The OFDM waveform is well suited for the 4G broadband access scenario, in which base stations are synchronized in time and frequency, and users are predominately served by one base station at a time. Uplink synchronization is realized by timing advance mechanisms controlled by the serving base station. Furthermore, macro and small cells are usually allocated a dedicated and contiguous part of the spectrum. However, with heterogeneous network deployments, where different cell sizes are combined, more spectrum allocation flexibility will be required. Therefore, new PHY and MAC functionalities to support asynchronous multi-connectivity, autonomous in-cluster self-organization of radio resources, spectrum coordination with other wireless communication clusters, and support for high mobility—possibly without wireless infrastructure support—will be required for 5G.

5G will support multiple point access to various base stations. This will make timing advances infeasible unless the involved base stations are operated at separate frequencies/PRBs. Multi-access-interference (MAI) will become a significant challenge in network design with OFDM applied. MAI and asynchronous signals will become particularly severe in network-assisted or ad-hoc vehicle-to-vehicle or vehicle-to-infrastructure wireless communication with several simultaneous links in a meshed topology.

Solutions being investigated and designed include new scalable waveforms to be configured in spectral localization, which need to be robust against timing jitter, and MAI, scalable in allocated system bandwidth per wireless link, access point, or wireless system and must support easy frequency domain equalization for frequency selective channels. Filter Bank Multicarrier (FBMC) is one promising candidate for a 5G physical layer (PHY). Nonorthogonal schemes for multi-user access (NOMA) are also under investigation; these consider channel overloading techniques for multi-user/multi-point communications, for example by a superposition of orthogonal waveforms

(CDMA, OFDMA) or specific nonorthogonal CDMA designs. The resulting interference between users can be handled by more complex signal processing on the receiver side.

One of the key differences between 4G and 5G networks is the spectrum extension beyond 6 GHz, which will allow significantly more bandwidth per wireless link and per base station. Furthermore, the interference range will be smaller than experienced below 6 GHz because of the need for more directional transmission of energy. This is caused by the link budget and the limited available transmit power. This makes mmWave wireless access the ideal candidate for small-cell deployments. In mmWave small cells deployments, the number of active users should shrink proportionally to the coverage area. TDMA can therefore be a sufficient solution for multiuser access. Beamforming antennas are seen as mandatory to reach the high gain (directionality) for dynamic outdoor environments. Furthermore, transmit power at mmWave is usually limited. Therefore, advanced multicarrier waveforms with low Peak-to-Average Power Ratio (PAPR) are crucial.

These technological directions are expected to be a key differentiator between the 4G and 5G cellular standards. 5G will introduce new transmitter and receiver designs, new modulation schemes and waveforms, new adaptive antenna array technologies for mmWave bands and new regulatory regulations on spectrum sharing, interference mitigation, and licensed and unlicensed operation.

References

1. Ericsson, "5G—What it is?" White Paper, October 2015;
2. http://www.streamingmediaglobal.com/Articles/News/Featured-News/Ericsson-Plans-5G-Showcase-at-2018-Winter-Olympics-105898.aspx
3. http://www.telegraph.co.uk/technology/news/10598874/South-Korea-to-invest-900m-in-5G-development.html
4. http://www.phonearena.com/news/Japans-NTT-DoCoMo-shares-its-plans-to-deliver-5G-in-time-for-the-Olympics-in-2020_id72473
5. 3GPP, SP-150149, "5G" timeline in 3GPP, http://www.3gpp.org/news-events/3gpp-news/1674-timeline_5g
6. NGMN Alliance, "NGMN 5G White Paper", February 2015;
7. GSMA Intelligence, "Understanding 5G: Perspectives on future technological advancements in mobile", December 2014;
8. Huawei, "5G: A Technology Vision", White Paper, November, 2013;
9. Ericsson, "5G - Requirements and capabilities", White Paper 2015;
10. Samsung Electronics, "5G Vision", White Paper, February 2015;
11. Nokia, "5G Use Cases and Requirements", White Paper, 2014;
12. 4G Americas, "Recommendation on 5G Requirements and Solutions", White Paper, October 2014;
13. 4G Americas, "Mobile Broadband Evolution towards 5G: Rel-12 & Rel-13 and beyond", White Paper, June 2015;
14. Markus D. Mueck, Ingolf Karls et.all, "Global Standards enabling a 5th Generation Communications System Architecture Vision", IEEE Globecom 2014, Workshop on Telecommunications Standards on Emerging Technologies for 5G Wireless Cellular Networks, Austin, Texas, USA;
15. 3GPP TR 38.900 "Study on channel model for frequency spectrum above 6 GHz" 2016

CHAPTER 4

▒ ▒ ▒

5G Technologies

As discussed in the previous chapter, the wireless communication ecosystem stakeholders are currently in the process of trying to figure out what will be the key 5G use cases, enabling everything from autonomously driving cars to 8K video streaming to the billions of connections characteristic of the Internet of Things (IoT). Recently published white papers by key stakeholders have revealed some mutual shared views on 5G requirements and key features.

First there is wireless access speed, important for extreme mobile broadband access (xMBB), where 5G will achieve peak data rates up to several times faster than LTE Advanced's peak speeds of 1 Gbps. In 5G laboratory trials peak speeds of 7.5 Gbps [1] or even 1 Tbps [2] have been achieved (a peak rate that shouldn't be expected in commercial networks). Second is capacity, which is important in particular for extreme machine-type communication (xMTC), where, for example, NGMN expects 5G to provide between 100 and 1,000 times more capacity than 4G [3]. These factors may seem excessive at a first glance, but current studies show that by 2019 alone the mobile capacity requirements will increase by a factor of 6-10 times compared to 2014 as shown in a recent overview published by GSMA [4], illustrated in Figure 4-1. Third, there is latency, important for extremely responsive and reliable machine-type communication. 5G must have a latency of a single millisecond, 50 times faster than 4G, or even less [1]. And finally, the network will run on either centimeter wave bands at spectrum frequencies below 6GHz or centimeter and millimeter wave bands above it. 5G networks shall consist of densely deployed indoor and outdoor small cells, new antenna designs including massive MIMO, combinations of multiple radio access technologies, including WiFi, and evolution of software defined networking (SDN) and network function virtualization (NFV) for better resource and energy efficiency.

© Intel Corp. 2016
B. Badic et al., *Rolling Out 5G*, DOI 10.1007/978-1-4842-1506-7_4

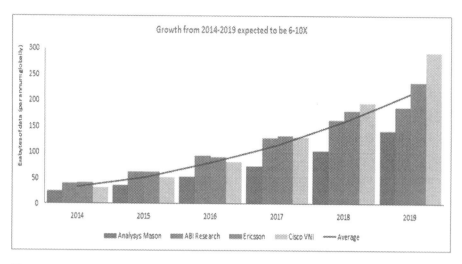

Figure 4-1. *Future mobile capacity requirements [1]*

5G Key Technologies

There are many questions surrounding 5G's key features, so here we will answer some important ones in an organized way to provide the most recent information on the progress of 5G. There are plentiful lively discussions on 5G's key features worldwide, and there are already many white papers from 5G related organizations. For example, ITU-R WP5D has published a timeline for IMT-2020 [5], and a first 3GPP 5G workshop took place in September, 2015 [6]. The requirements and technical discussions regarding key features have started and are going to converge most likely in 2016 (as shown in Figures 3-1 and 3-2 in Chapter 3). Hence, it is necessary to elaborate not only on key 5G features as such but also on related technical aspects.

So where to start elaborating on 5G key features? There is always the typical industry buzz at the hype cycle's beginning, with plenty of press releases, company announcements, and many other things about 5G key features. And many of you may wonder why the time is right now for 5G. Looking at the evolution and revolution of wireless communication technology over time, one recognizes that it will take a long time to get a next generation of communication technology right and to make sure that there is proper standardization and regulation to create the wireless industry ecosystems we all enjoy. Looking at Figure 4-2, we see a 10-year period between the major wireless communication technology generations.

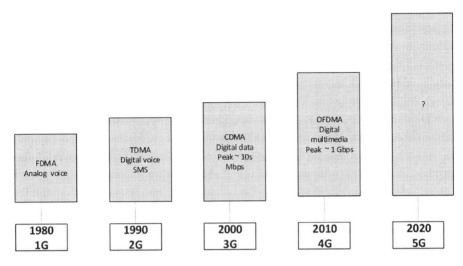

Figure 4-2. *Evolution of network generations*

As we discussed in the previous chapter, the timing is right for communication ecosystem stakeholders to start to work diligently together on the next wireless communication technology for 2020. Nevertheless, it is clear that there is still a lot of headroom for the 4G cellular standard to improve. There are currently more than 425 commercial LTE networks in 145 countries worldwide, with already 88 LTE-Advanced commercial networks in 45 countries [7]. LTE is one of the fastest-growing mobile broadband communication technologies in the world and will reach nearly 1 billion connections in 2015 and 3.6 billion in 2020 [8].

As discussed in Chapter 3, the technology roadmap of 4G still has many innovative key features to be deployed in the next few years. One key feature to be implemented is carrier aggregation (CA). Other features target flexibility, like enhanced support for HetNets, more advanced antenna features and 256 QAM, as well as higher capacity for machine-type-communication (MTC). Communication system performance will be further improved by better device interference cancellation, along with coordinated multipoint (CoMP) for cell edge and self-organizing networks (SON). Features like LTE Broadcast, LTE Direct, D2D, new spectrum bands, and new licensing models will allow network operators and other ecosystem stakeholders to build innovative services for their customers with many more awesome technical features in the years to come.

The wireless communication ecosystem is an incredible industry that is growing rapidly at the mobile broadband demand rate of 57 % per year [9], which is both a challenge and an opportunity. How does one meet this mobile broadband demand, not only from computers, tablets, and smartphones, but also the coming IoT devices? Getting the right answer means increasing capacity, increasing efficiency, increasing adaptability, and finally increasing innovation with 5G. The answer to the broadband challenge requires massive traffic capacity, higher downlink and uplink speeds, better spectrum efficiency, and the flexibility to use new spectrum. In addition, the IoT will need to support billions of connections, with reduced signaling and low energy consumption, and its mission-critical services need very low latency, high reliability, high availability, and very secure connections. It is immediately clear that addressing all these needs will unleash new powerful innovative applications and very creative use cases.

Looking at where the wireless communication ecosystem is today and what needs to be done, it is evident that it is going to take time. There is a lot of work to be done for 5G, specifically in 3GPP but many other standards-developing organizations (SDOs) as well. Hence the commercial rollout of 5G technologies is expected in the 2020 time frame or beyond. At the same time, 4G will continue to progress, continuing to be the basic mobile broadband foundation even as 5G begins to be deployed (Figure 3-1, Chapter 3).

Spectrum Management Vectors

One important change that 5G will introduce is related to spectrum. If we look at how mobile operators and their ecosystem partners serve their customers, it is about technology evolution and revolution married with spectrum.

Figure 4-3 illustrates different and complementary approaches for making more spectrum available:

- *Higher Frequencies*: There is currently a trend to exploit frequencies above 6 GHz, in particular in the centimeter and millimeter wave bands. Corresponding solutions require a substantial amount of innovation but provide the potential for GHz bandwidths to be made available for mobile applications.

- *Spectrum Sharing*: Because of the lack of spectrum in traditional mobile wireless bands below 6 GHz, regulation authorities are starting to consider alternative ways to manage spectrum availability. Spectrum-sharing technologies have been introduced in Europe (Licensed Shared Access in 2.3-2.4 GHz) and the US (Spectrum Access System in 3.55–3.7 GHz) and are expected to be applied to further bands in the future. The new technologies will enable wireless broadband applications to exploit bands that are allocated to different incumbents. Such bands are often lightly used over geographic areas and times and thus provide a large potential for being used on a co-primary basis by wireless broadband stakeholders. In the future, sharing strategies may also be applied to higher-frequency bands in the centimeter and millimeter wave range.

- *Spectral Efficiency*: It is a never-ending story to improve wireless communication systems further in order to minimize the required bandwidth for delivering a given level of service quality. Recent trends include advanced MIMO schemes, higher-order modulation, reduction of signaling overhead, improved interaction between heterogeneous networks, and the like. Any improvement in spectral efficiency allows reducing the required amount of spectrum to be allocated to a single specific user— indirectly leading to more spectrum being available and allowing more users to be served at their target service quality.

- *Densification*: It is a clear trend in 5G communication systems to bring the mobile users closer to the base stations, in particular by deploying a dense network of small cells. This leads to improved radio link characteristics (thanks to a smaller communication range) and a smaller number of users to be served by a given cell (thanks to the reduced range of a small cell). Again, this technology thus indirectly allows additional spectrum resources to be allocated to users.

All of the approaches just discussed are independent of each other and thus can be combined to see corresponding gains multiply, as illustrated in Figure 4-3.

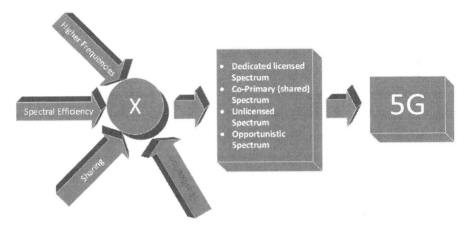

Figure 4-3. *Vectors for 5G capacity*

Depending on the inherent band requirements, the final frequency allocation can be as follows:

- *Dedicated licensed spectrum*: This is the classical type of spectrum being used by cellular carriers. The spectrum is auctioned and then made available on an exclusively licensed basis. No sharing with other stakeholders is required.

- *Co-Primary (shared) spectrum*: The Licensed Shared Access and Spectrum Access System spectrum sharing strategies provide access to a Co-Primary spectrum. Licensees typically negotiate with existing incumbents in order to agree on a Sharing Agreement that enables Licensees, such as cellular carriers, to use the shared bands for capacity extension of their existing networks while the incumbent is absent.

- *Unlicensed Spectrum:* Unlicensed spectrum is mainly used to provide low-cost spectrum access to technologies such as WiFi and 3GPP License Assisted Access. It is expected that unlicensed spectrum will further be available in the future. The FCC, for example, introduces a quasi-unlicensed regime for tier-3 users (General Authorized Access) in the Spectrum Access System technology for spectrum sharing.

- *Opportunistic Spectrum:* In the case of highly dynamic incumbents, opportunistic usage approaches allow secondary users to access the spectrum whenever it is available—even if it may only be during short periods of time. Currently opportunistic access technologies play hardly any role in commercial broadband communications. They may be potential candidates for the future when spectrum becomes increasingly scarce and even small spectrum opportunities must be exploited.

Radio Access

One key characteristic of 5G will be new radio access technology architecture. What are the radio access technology candidates for 5G, and is there really a new radio access technology needed? Answering these questions will be demanding and leads immediately to another one: what is a new radio access technology? When a network went from 3G to 4G the answer was simple, since one had mostly to decide between modulations and coding. There were the TDMA versus CDMA and the CDMA versus OFDM battles. But for 5G there are much more difficult decisions now. There are three obvious main drivers for this new radio access technology that is coming.

First it is about *spectrum.* While 5G will certainly work in the existing cellular bands as well, there are also completely new bands that are required. For example, the 15 kHz spacing for subcarriers used today would be very inappropriate for a contiguous bandwidth of 1 GHz at millimeter wave bands from a signal processing perspective. So better solutions are needed here. Next it is about *services.* Each of the predecessor generations targeted a main single use case and service, which then became a subset of the successor generation for backward compatibility. 2G started with digital voice, 3G went to multimedia, and then 4G to mobile broadband. For 5G around a hundred use cases have already been gathered, with three identified as extremes: the xMBB, the extreme machine type services (eMTC), and the very latency-sensitive services. This is definitely a much wider set of requirements than in the previous generations. Third, 5G is about a greatly *increased interdependency* between the radio access technology and the core network because the end-to-end capabilities of the network become much more important. Therefore it can be concluded that the 5G radio access technology is going to be something different than the previous generations.

Looking at the complexity of the use cases and services and their extremes in a bit more detail, one sees even more clearly that a new radio access technology is needed. For example, the LTE waveform is probably not well suited for millimeter wave bands, targeting very high data throughputs for xMBB in nomadic use cases. (Otherwise, however, 5G can reuse 4G capacity when it comes to reliable coverage.) For eMTC, LTE as of early 2016 is not well suited, either. It can transmit small data packets, but these transmissions are not as efficient as broadband streams. As a result, massive IoT data is going to sacrifice spectrum efficiency; this will lead to the requirement of something new.

Another issue is consistency. For example, there is a great difference between the user experience at the cell edge and in the center of a cell. Again looking at xMBB applications like video streaming, the 100 Mbps average is much more important for the user than the peak performance. With LTE technology today this most likely cannot be done yet. Adding massive MIMO might help to achieve those average rates needed at the cell edge for a good video streaming experience, but it requires new pilot structures, better user differentiation leading to specific control, and finally changing the radio access technology. Finally, the LTE radio access technology dictates the minimum latency as of today, even moving the application to the network edge. Services that are mission-critical, such as Vehicle to X communication (V2X), require a much shorter round trip time (RTT) and connectionless mode, which once again cannot be done with today's LTE. So a new 5G radio access technology will gracefully incorporate the existing 4G with new modulation, coding, and MAC schemes. The objective is to deliver, instead of more dumb bits, better and smarter bits as the basis for more intelligent services.

Context-Aware Networking

Context-aware networking is another technology concept that 5G will incorporate to increase network efficiency, providing seamless service delivery and the best user experience, at the right time and with the right means. *Context* is defined here as the availability of a number of alternate radio access technologies and of both small cell networks and macro networks. From a device point of view, context means making intelligent devices aware of associated service requirements to align the subscription context with operator preferences by exploiting service and subscriber analytics. Context awareness allows the network to adapt dynamically to any kind of devices and services rather than the devices and services adapting to the network (the one-size-fits-all-network access available today). The network will adapt to the needs of the devices and services within a framework of policies and within its context. For example, a set of stationary IoT devices do not need a network that supports mobility, like 3GPP Mobility Management and paging. Only device-initiated communication is required. Here, optimizing the resource allocation will make networks simpler and reduce cost.

ITU-R WP5D, Revision 2 to Document 5D/TEMP/469-E, Chapter 5.3.8 describes context awareness as delivering context information in real time about the network, devices, applications, and the user and her environment to application and network layers in the context of IMT-2020. This context is classified as device-level (for example, battery state and processing load), user (quality of experience preferences, activities, location, and mobility status), environment (devices in neighborhood, topology, background activities, and weather) or network (load, throughput, reliability, supported radio technologies, interference, and spectrum availability). 3GPP Release 13 already also provides context data as information elements; for example, the UE power preference indicator (PPI) assists base stations (BSes) in correctly configuring discontinuous reception (DRX) values, and there are reference signal received power and reference signal received quality (RSRP/RSRQ) measurements for serving and neighboring cells. But with the dense and widespread deployment of small cells there will be additional challenges—in particular, how to exploit the huge amount of user data for radio resource allocation in heterogeneous 5G networks in the most efficient way?

The evolving new radio management for LTE-Advanced Pro [10] and new 5G air interfaces will definitely have an influence on BS and UE measurements to collect context data for efficiently controlling the radio environment and therefore the spectrum resources. The BS has to measure timing advance (TA), average receive strength signal indicator (RSSI), average signal-to-interference-plus-noise ratio (SINR), uplink channel state information (UL CSI), detected physical random access channel (PRACH) preambles and transport channel block error ratio (BLER) for intra LTE today. The UE must measure channel quality indication (CQI), RSRP, and RSRQ. Further measurements are mainly for UE hand over (HO); these are for UMTS terrestrial radio access frequency division duplex (UTRA FDD) the following: common pilot channel received signal code power (CPICH RSCP), CPICH Ec/No carrier RSSI, and GSM carrier RSSI; for UMTS terrestrial radio access time division multiplex (UTRA TDD) they are carrier RSSI, RSCP, and primary common control physical channel (P-CCPCH), and for CMDA2000 they are 1x radio transmission technology (1xRTT) and high rate packet data (HRPD) pilot strength. And there might be more. LTE-Advanced Pro and the new 5G air interfaces (AIF) are going to increase considerably this impact raising new challenges to the UE performance and power budget.

Context data will be gathered by UE and macro network BSes and small cell BSes, locally sensing data to be sent to specific databases in the network and to be exploited by extended and new resource management algorithms. The amount of data to be gathered and the complexity of resource management algorithms need to be balanced very carefully between the network performance enhancements they will make available and the load they will impose on both the BS/AP and the UE in data gathering, signaling, processing, and storage. Effective and efficient support is needed for fast radio resource management, in particular for small-cell network deployments and dual- and multi-connectivity.

Radio resource management has an important role in wireless network operation, particularly in controlling the allocation and usage of available spectrum resources. LTE-Advanced Pro and the new 5G air interfaces will serve as building blocks of heterogeneous networks and will significantly increase this control complexity as they rely more on sensing, transmitting, storing, and receiving context information in UEs and eNodeBs. Related specifications in ITU-R (for context definition), 3GPP RAN (for measurement definition and measurement gaps) and SA (testing) will be investigated for changes needed.

Millimeter Wave Technology

There is a lot of talk about millimeter wave technology as one of the key technology enablers for 5G, particularly as part of the quest for more spectrum. And there are still major technical challenges to overcome for the utilization of radio access technology for millimeter wave bands. What are they? In general, using higher-frequency bands presents both technical and deployment hurdles to be resolved. Millimeter wave bands (and to certain extent centimeter bands above 6 GHz) have unfortunately poor propagation, penetration, and diffraction characteristics compared to current cellular radio access technologies. So new technologies are needed to overcome these drawbacks, which is the impetus for current research and development of massive MIMO and beamforming (BF) technology, for example. After the technology is developed, the challenge becomes providing cost-effective, consumer-grade products. That will take some time, because the semiconductor chipset suppliers have to provide components. Furthermore, there is a close relationship between the technical challenge and the deployment challenge. In millimeter wave implementations, there is the issue of blockage caused by stationery buildings or foliage like trees, that caused by moving objects like cars and people between the BS and UE, and even worse, self-induced blockage due to the human body of the user. That means communication needs mostly line of sight (LoS) or near LoS between BS and UE plus a strong non-line of sight (NLOS) path. Consequently, the UE needs to be connected to at least two BSes to make sure there is connectivity. On top of that, one needs a link budget that allows distances of up to 100 m instead of kilometers, which means again a lot of base stations to be deployed. But where to put them? The conclusion is that operators need to define ways to deploy a large number of small-cell BSes most efficiently.

Millimeter wave technology is explained in detail in Chapter 6.

Device-to-Device Communication

Device-to-Device (D2D) communication was standardized in 3GPP LTE Release 12 as LTE Device to Device Proximity Services (ProSe). The key purpose of the feature is to enable mobile devices to discover the presence of other nearby devices within the range of up to 500 m and communicate with them directly with minimal support from the network. Exploiting direct communication between devices improves spectrum utilization, overall throughput, and energy consumption, while providing new peer-to-peer and proximity-based applications and services (Figure 4-4).

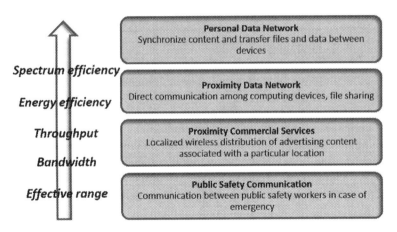

Figure 4-4. ProSe use cases and benefits

The basic D2D procedure shown in Figure 4-5 consists of three steps:

1. *Device discovery (ProSe Discovery):* Detecting the presence of other devices in the neighborhood.

2. *Link setup:* Establishing links between interested devices.

3. *Data communication (ProSe Communication):* Transmitting or receiving data via established links.

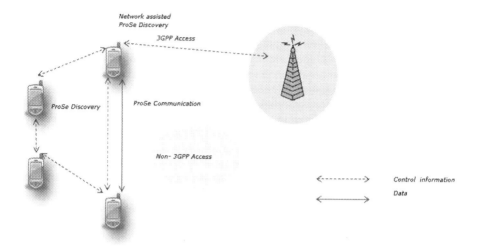

Figure 4-5. *Basic ProSe procedure*

ProSe Discovery is a process that identifies when a UE is in the proximity of another UE, using E-UTRA (evolved UMTS Terrestrial Radio Access); that is, it enables a mobile device to use the LTE air interface to discover other D2D-capable devices in its proximity and, if permitted, to discover certain information about them. Therefore, in permission terms, ProSe Discovery can be classified as both restricted and open-discovery. The use of ProSe Discovery must be authorized by the operator, and the authorization can be on a per-UE or per-UE-per-application basis. An authorized application can interact with the ProSe Discovery feature to request the use of certain ProSe Discovery preferences. The network controls the use of E-UTRA resources used for ProSe Discovery for a ProSe-enabled UE. ProSe Discovery can be used as a standalone process (that is, it is not necessarily followed by ProSe Communication) or as an enabler of other services.

ProSe Communication is communication between two UEs in proximity by means of an E-UTRAN communication path established between the UEs. The communication path can be established directly between the UEs or routed via a local eNB(s). The use of ProSe Communication must be authorized by the operator. Unless explicitly stated otherwise, the term "ProSe Communication" refers to any or all of the following: ProSe E-UTRA Communication between only two ProSe-enabled UEs; ProSe Group Communication or ProSe Broadcast Communication among Public Safety ProSe-enabled UEs; and ProSe-assisted WLAN direct communication.

Vehicle to X Communication

Vehicle-to-Vehicle communication, Advanced Driver Assistance Systems (ADAS), and Autonomous Vehicles are emerging trends in the automotive field. Additionally, increased traffic is becoming a major issue in cities, leading to productivity loss, pollution, and poor quality of life. 3GPP has created a Study Item, V2X, within SA1, TR 22.885, that will define use cases and requirements to support communication between vehicles. V2X communication is any exchange of information between a vehicle and any entity that may affect the vehicle, and vice versa. The X can be for example another vehicle (V), infrastructure (I), pedestrian (P), home (H), or any other entity communicating with the vehicle (Figure 4-6).

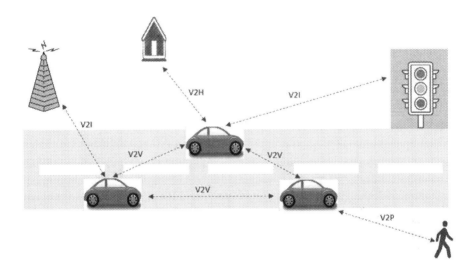

Figure 4-6. *V2X communication*

V2X use cases are not defined yet, but as shown in Figure 4-7 and discussed at [8], information exchanged in V2X will be used for safety, mobility, and environmental applications, including driver assistance, speed control, emergency information, navigation, traffic operations and demand management, personal navigation, signs, road payment transactions, and so on. Thus there is a significant commercial value and benefit for society in enabling V2X communication.

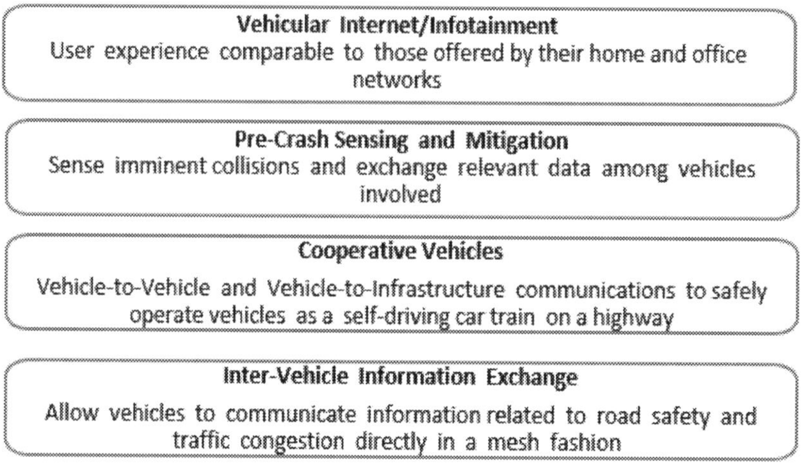

Vehicular Internet/Infotainment
User experience comparable to those offered by their home and office networks

Pre-Crash Sensing and Mitigation
Sense imminent collisions and exchange relevant data among vehicles involved

Cooperative Vehicles
Vehicle-to-Vehicle and Vehicle-to-Infrastructure communications to safely operate vehicles as a self-driving car train on a highway

Inter-Vehicle Information Exchange
Allow vehicles to communicate information related to road safety and traffic congestion directly in a mesh fashion

Figure 4-7. *V2X use cases*

Heterogeneous Networks Using Multiple Air Interfaces

LTE and IEEE 802.11 (WiFi) interworking is becoming ubiquitous, a trend driven by smartphones and tablets that are equipped with both air interfaces, making heterogeneous networks using multiple air interfaces a reality. But having both air interfaces up and running does not mean today that there are any of the following features: a simple and automatic air interface access selection, single authentication, easy air interface aggregation, or seamless mobility and roaming. LTE, 802.11, and the new 802.11ad (WiGig) have little in common, having been standardized by different bodies (3GPP and IEEE), and their radio access and network functions differ considerably. Data routing under IEEE 802.11 is controlled by the device and not the network; its model is not information-centric networking. So going from dual-connectivity to multi-connectivity and supporting multiple air interfaces, even those from different camps, will dramatically improve operational efficiency and user experience.

The 5G system needs to be easy to deploy, scalable, flexible and cost- and energy-efficient. Thanks to the gains they provide, heterogeneous networks will play a crucial role in 5G systems; they will implement the concepts of dual and multiple connectivity by using existing and new air interfaces for radio access. Heterogeneous networks can improve network system throughput considerably, which is urgently needed to deal with the relentlessly rising data demand. Heterogeneous networks are the solution for small-cell underlay in a macro-cell network, as they can dynamically support the extremely high data capacities needed in hot spots. Small cells are an essential part of a heterogeneous network and greatly enhance spectrum efficiency. Small cells provide extreme mobile broadband capacity for nomadic user equipment, offloading macro cells that deliver the most reliable coverage for moving UEs and IoT.

However, heterogeneous networks face challenges in network management and energy efficiency. Many small cells together increase exponentially the number of cell selection, reselection, and handover events and therefore the system signaling complexity compared to macro cells. Large differences in the transmit power of small- and macro-cell base stations disturb the performance of cell edge UEs considerably and degrade the network's mobility management. Small-cell stations are to be switched on and off according to data capacity demand in time and area. This adds to the network management complexity as well.

The Control Plane / User Plane Split

An early concept of a heterogeneous network configuration with control plane (C-plane) and user plane (U-plane) split was published by Ericsson [11], proposing network-centric soft-cell schemes to meet data rate and capacity demands. Another heterogeneous network concept, deploying phantom cells as small cells at different frequency bands than the macro cells, was proposed by NTT DoCoMo [12]. The MiWEBA research project [13] from the European Union's Seventh Framework Program expedited this idea by studying heterogeneous networks comprising LTE macro cells and small cells and a millimeter wave small-cell underlay. METIS 2020 [14] envisaged for UDN/macro integration a potential split of control and user planes as well, and METIS II [15], its successor, focuses on a split of control and user planes in certain communication and deployment scenarios; for example, as one fundamental design aspect related to 5G RAN design. Intel explored the data rate improvement in particular in the uplink (UL) data bearer split in terms of user throughput gain and network load balancing between macro BS and small cell BS in [16]. And in [17], an extended U- and C-plane architecture for tightly coupled LTE WiGig interworking implementing a LTE millimeter wave heterogeneous network is proposed, which shows in simulations a significantly increased user data rate.

Some of the fundamental challenges of small-cell underlay, such as the maintenance of mobility and connectivity, are addressed by using a C- and U-plane split. So it is no surprise that heterogeneous network architecture concepts (Figures 4-8, 4-9) as solutions to 5G system needs currently have a lot of momentum. Exploiting heterogeneous network gains and overcoming the shortcomings of small-cell underlays leads to a networking architecture with control and user plane split (3GPP), where a common C-plane controls the radio access of a UE with multiple air interfaces.

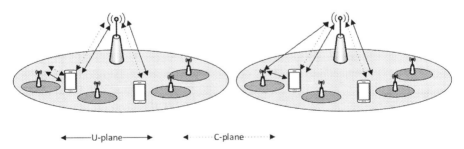

Figure 4-8. *Heterogeneous network scenario without (left) and with (right) C-plane and U-plane split*

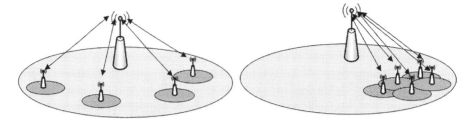

Figure 4-9. *Sparsely (left) and densely (right) small cell deployment*

A common type of C-plane using a common air interface transmits acquisition and reference signals and system information. The air interface used covers a wide area and is very reliable and energy-efficient. The C-plane establishes, alters, and releases the UE radio resource control (RRC) layers. It deals with the network-controlled mobility and conveys the measurement and configuration reporting. The different user planes (U-plane) supporting multiple air interfaces handle UE data transmission, covering the packet data convergence protocol (PDCP), radio link control (RLC), and media access control (MAC). This setup overcomes the drawbacks of small-cell underlays and achieves the highest flexibility, scalability, and reliability by supporting a huge variety of deployment and data rate scenarios.

An example of architecture supporting macro- and small-cell dual connectivity in an LTE-Advanced heterogeneous network is given in [18].

Wireless Backhauling

The LTE and LTE-Advanced network deployment already requires an increase in system throughput, low latency, and flexibility as it implements, for example, 3GPP Release 10 carrier aggregation (CA) and 3GPP Release 11 coordinate multipoint (CoMP) for wireless backhaul. ETSI ISG mWT addresses a major increase in data throughput, range, spectrum efficiency, and service reliability, with a corresponding decrease in latency, jitter, and power consumption, as well improvements in security, setup, and maintenance. Backhaul data traffic involves user data, S1 protocol data, X2 handover data, and management and synchronization data. The latter two are minor compared to the previous ones. Macro cell wireless backhaul with point-to-point (P2P) line-of-sight (LOS) links is used to provide data throughput between 400 Mbps and 2 Gbps over distances up to 5 km in spectra above 6 GHz, including the millimeter band above 30 GHz [19]. Recently wireless backhaul went into the 70-80 GHz spectrum (E-band), where the data throughput can reach up to 5 Gbps [19].

Small cells are the next target application, where the wireless backhaul provides single- and multi-hop links from fiber to small-cell BSes. Link distances are up to 500 meters in certain cases, whereas the links could be both LOS and non-line-of-sight (NLOS). Spectrum between 6 and 100 GHz is being investigated, including in-band solutions where the backhaul is operating in the same spectrum as the access. There is also a new type of remote radio head (RRH) being linked flexibly into the system, for example via wireless front-haul links. The protocols transmitted over a front haul are CPRI and OBSAI, with raw data throughput up to 60 and 70 Gbps for LTE and up to 100 Gbps for LTE-A/ JT-CoMP [20].

The use of centimeter and millimeter bands provides opportunities for deploying front-haul and backhaul links in several scenarios [21]. LTE-Advanced Pro and new 5G air interfaces are anticipated to realize gigabit-level system throughput. However, this creates tremendous challenges to the backhaul, which must flexibly feed the radio access network in an efficient and effective way. Among the concepts to be investigated are the use of millimeter wave bands for wireless backhaul and front haul in different scenarios [22], as in Figure 4-10.

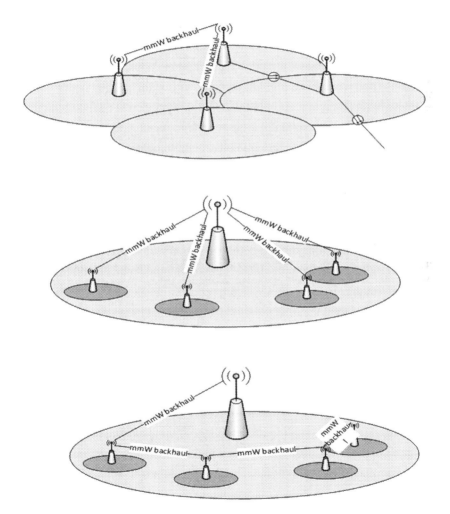

Figure 4-10. *Typical wireless backhaul scenarios*

Networking and Virtualization Approaches

With the opportunity of 5G new challenges arise. The network operator's present business model is becoming exposed. The demand for bandwidth required by subscribers is growing faster than the revenue generated from connectivity and services. It is important to launch new business models and to bring to the table new technologies to build out network capacity that meets the requirements of the market while also being profitable. Gradually, network architectures must become more flexible, efficient, and scalable to accommodate the rapid growth in data traffic and the number and variety of connected devices in the IoT. Therefore, network operators are restlessly focused on increasing capital expenditure (CAPEX) efficiency, improving operational expenditure (OPEX) like consumption of electricity, and managing the network and the quick deployment of new applications and services. All of this needs to be done to continue to improve user experience quality.

Software-defined networking (SDN) is an approach to networking that is characterized by a decoupling of control and forwarding functions, enabling simplified operations, heightened automation, improved resource efficiency, and on-demand network programmability. Network function virtualization (NFV) is the deployment and delivery of networking services via software systems executing as server-based processes. These server-based software systems directly replace traditional physical networking appliances (such as WAN optimization) and devices (such as routers). NFV uses standard IT virtualization technology to migrate these fixed-function boxes to software applications on, for example, a commercial off-the-shelf (COTS) Intel architecture-based (IA) server, which can host multiple virtual network functions. Similarly, fixed-function devices such as firewalls, load balancers, and intrusion detection systems can be replaced with a COTS server running these network functions in software. The server is enabled to become the new networking device by moving from today's traditional networking topology, with monolithic vertical integrated boxes and telecom equipment manufacturers (TEM) providing proprietary solutions, toward networking within virtual machines (VMs) running on standard IA server hardware and open standard solutions (Figure 4-11).

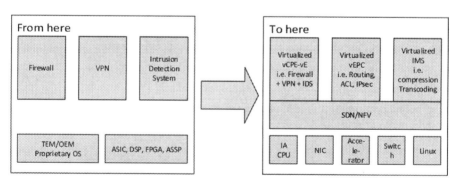

Server gets enabled to become the networking device.

Figure 4-11. SDN and NFV drive network transformation

NFV is about dynamic provisioning of services and virtualizing network applications and network service functions such as those now provided by dedicated core network components, media servers, and radio access management functions on general-purpose servers (VMs). The services run on hypervisors in VMs using shared, off-the-shelf data center computing infrastructure, independent of physical network topology. The transition toward an SND and NFC as the new normal has started, as NFV is already employed in 4G implementations and will be commonplace well before 5G. But key challenges like missing or incomplete standards, technology immaturity, and imprecise cost/benefit tradeoffs remain. For example, Intel's open approach through industry open source and standards like ETSI, NFV, and MEC contributes to solutions and accelerates SDN and NFV adoption by providing reference architecture servers for SND and NFV. Going forward, NFV can be exploited as a technology fundamental to the design of 5G, where we expect the majority of the wireless network functions in the RAN and the core to be virtualized, thus increasing flexibility to meet varied demands on control and data processing from a large variety of applications.

Whereas most of the mobile network virtualization effort so far has been focused on moving core network functions to data centers in the cloud, mobile edge computing (MEC), illustrated in Figure 4-12, offers another method of exploiting virtualization technologies within a 5G core and radio access network. It will allow additional opportunities for cost savings for mobile operators and wireless communication ecosystem partners by tight interworking of data communication, processing, storage, and management capabilities very near the radio access nodes. Some of the 5G requirements, like data throughput for the extreme mobile broadband and low latency for V2X, will benefit from MEC, which is also driven by the shift in 5G systems from purely coverage-driven wireless networks toward more capacity-driven networks and the request for a flexible and affordable network densification thereof. MEC will run on general-purpose processors (GPP) that are similar to those used in the data centers of SNDs and NFVs, but within the cloud MEC they will be very close to the radio edge or even within it, typically inside the BS or in its close proximity. A proof of concept is Cisco's EdgeCloud Smart Cell solution, based on Intel Core or Atom processor with around 40 Gbps, 4 GB of RAM, and 40 GB of flash memory.

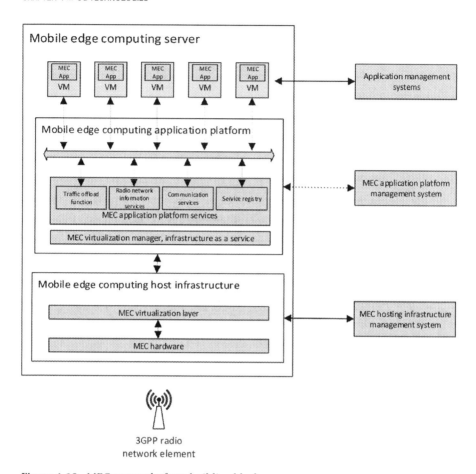

Figure 4-12. *MEC server platform building blocks*

ETSI now has the MEC ISG working on the standardization of MEC building blocks like platform services and APIs [30], virtual machine service level agreements (SLA), and the MEC application platform management interface, shown in Figure 4-12. Future releases after 2016 may include the integration with mobile core functions, additional radio and network information exposure, interfaces for orchestration functions, and support for network sharing.

5G will enable a range of new user experiences such as self-driving automobiles with intelligent traffic routing, smart cities, connected health innovations, and more using wireless links to IoT devices and to cloud-based computing and data services, calling for new approaches to network and device design. 5G will not be solely about increasing speed and capacity, but will also be about intelligence throughout the core network (CN) and the radio access network (RAN) to enable devices and the network to communicate more efficiently, transport data and content more quickly, and share computing and communication resources more efficiently. C- and U-plane splitting is a precondition for applying SDN and NFV. The virtualizing environment expands this by using, for example,

OpenStack and leveraged SDN solutions to expose the core networking and radio access network elements in a programmable manner.

The OpenStack community is a global partnership that is supported by many companies and organizations, with more than 18,000 members and 1300 active contributors to bring into being an open standard cloud computing platform [32]. OpenStack itself is a massively scalable, open cloud computing platform intended for setting up and running public, private, and hybrid cloud solutions through a single control plane. This open-source project has progressed quickly, and many early adopters, including Intel, are using it to organize large pools of computing, storage, and networking resources. For example, more details about how to develop flexible cloud networking solutions as defined by SDN and NFV with Intel Open Network Platform Server (Intel ONP Server) Reference Architecture (RA) can be found at [33].

The network operators will perceive agility as a key thing.

All system parts—core network, radio access network, and devices linked to them—will interwork to establish intelligent service awareness. All service-related actions of 5G system parts will be scheduled based on device and network context to create system flexibility that will cope efficiently with the various device connectivity, processing, power, latency, and cost requirements. The 5G system will be forward-compliant, supporting device evolution in size, form, function, computing, and communication capabilities. Its core network and radio access network must intelligently manage network access in a dynamic manner, taking care of gathering, sharing, storing, and processing contextual data from all system elements.

Mobile networks have embraced the Internet for more than 20 years, but they are still very different in the way they deal with support for new uses cases and scenarios compared to the Internet. Adding new capabilities and functions in mobile networks becomes more and more costly because of further complexity. Along with backward compatibility, forward compatibility becomes urgent in mobile radio access and network functions, to provide mobility, flexibility, scalability, reliability, security and slenderness.

The innovation in computing and storage fuels developments in SDN as well as NFV and is even expected to accelerate the progress there. It is about network programmability and configurability, including network slicing and policy framework. There are still a lot of open questions, such as what functions will be integrated—even wireless control functions like mobility management, security, and charging [8]. The answers to those questions will probably have a huge influence on the core network and the radio access network. For example, consider a logical instance or layer that is going to set up and coordinate resources for and among multiple air interfaces. This control unit would be able to assist network function virtualization by allowing the instantiation of core and radio access network functions on demand without having to alter the network system. Finally, SDN methods will allow (closely associated and corresponding to NFV) to deploy and manage automatically network functions and systems. The ETSI NFC MANO working group, for example, is defining such a control and orchestration framework for 4G, which could be the foundation for the evolution of LTE Advanced and 5G as well.

NFV, SDN, and MEC are based on the separation of C-plane and U-plane, network abstraction and programmability of core and radio access network and are designed to be generally applicable to 5G systems, enabling innovative services and reducing the time and effort to implement, run, and maintain them. All of these technologies will allow network operators and regulators to match requests for applications and services dynamically by setting up and shifting 5G system resources in such a way that they efficiently match these requirements. CAPEX and OPEX savings will come from replacing proprietary hardware by NFV running core and radio access network functions in data centers. NFV, SDN, and MEC with centralized network functions provide a much tighter integration between base stations and enhanced signaling and will drive the path to better network performance as well. Examples include the adoption of LTE-A features like coordinated multi-point (CoMP), enhanced inter-cell interference coordination (eICIC), and 3D MIMO.

Opportunistic/Moving Networks

Opportunistic Networks (ONs) have been introduced by [24,25]. These are operator-governed, temporary, and coordinated extensions of an existing network infrastructure. These extensions are dynamically created, through operator spectrum, policies, information, and knowledge, in places and at the time they are needed to deliver multimedia flows to mobile users in a most efficient manner. They can comprise network elements of the infrastructure, and terminals/devices, potentially organized without infrastructure, that are opportunistically exploiting the available resources (communication, computing, and storage).

Opportunistic networks typically exist for a particular time interval, needed for application provision to users in the most efficient manner, and go through the following life-cycle:

1. *ON Suitability Determination*: Detection of opportunities with respect to nodes and potential radio paths, assessment of potential gains

2. *ON Creation*: Selection of nodes, selection of links/RATs/ spectrum, selection of routes

3. *ON Maintenance*: ON monitoring, ON reconfiguration

4. *ON Termination*: Cessation of application provisioning, inadequate gains or being forced

The key applications and use cases are illustrated below:

1. *Opportunistic coverage extension*:

    The network operator is enabled to provide extended coverage, for example to mobile device users located in remote areas. Direct connections to other mobile devices are exploited to relay the information into the coverage area of a wireless broadband network, typically a cellular network. Then the relayed information is provided to the concerned BS and AP and further transported to its intended destination (Figure 4-13).

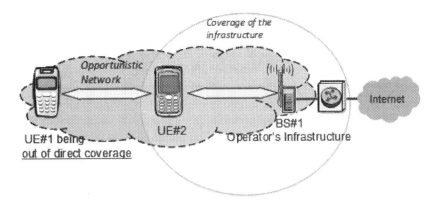

Figure 4-13. *Opportunistic coverage extension*

2. *Opportunistic capacity extension*:

Devices may receive additional capacity by maintaining multiple connections simultaneously. One link is typically established with a base station or access point, and the second link is provided through suitable relaying to nearby network infrastructure (Figure 4-14).

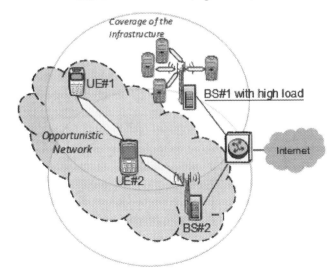

Figure 4-14. *Opportunistic capacity extension*

3. *Infrastructure-supported opportunistic ad-hoc networking:*

    Mobile devices are able to exchange user data directly through
    a device-to-device link. The control information, however,
    is still managed through the network infrastructure, which
    enables the network operator to ensure an efficient overall
    network configuration (Figure 4-15).

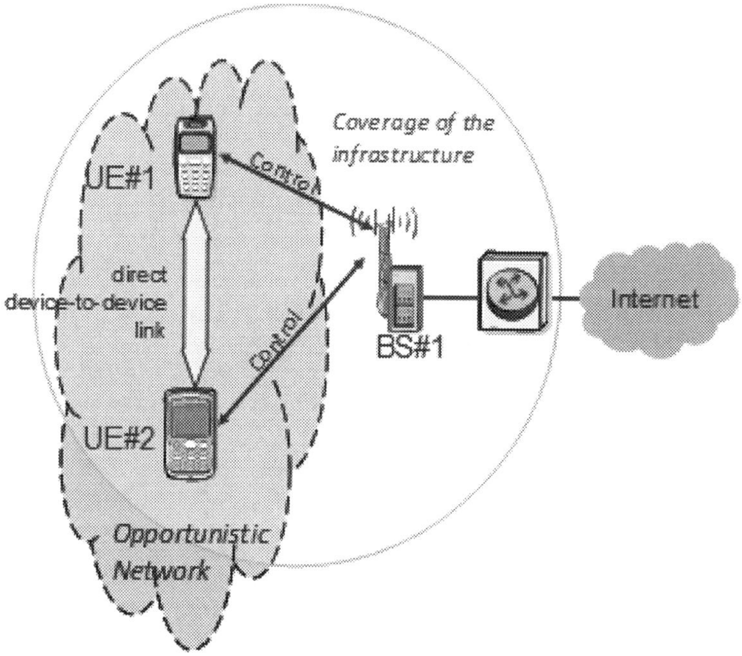

Figure 4-15. *Infrastructure-supported opportunistic ad-hoc networking*

4. *Opportunistic traffic aggregation in the radio access network:*

To minimize the communication distances between the
various mobile devices in a network, a given mobile device
serves as an aggregation point closely located to other tiers.
The aggregated information is then communicated to and
from the concerned network infrastructure, which finally
optimizes the overall power efficiency (Figure 4-16).

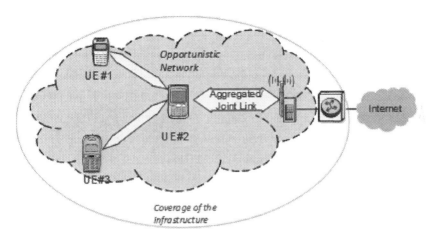

Figure 4-16. *Opportunistic traffic aggregation in the radio access network*

5. *Opportunistic resource aggregation in the backhaul network:*

If any network equipment has issues with the concerned
backhaul link (such as a broken or congested link), the
backhaul information is relayed through neighboring network
equipment. For this purpose, a point-to-point wireless link
is established between neighboring network equipment
(Figure 4-17).

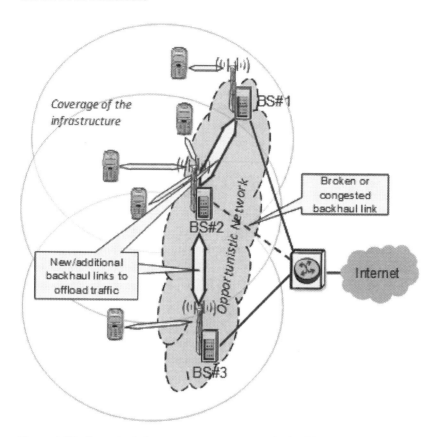

Figure 4-17. *Opportunistic resource aggregation in the backhaul network*

Open Source Software

Open source software is expected to play a major role in future 5G systems. The main applications are as follows:

i. Adaptation of generic equipment platforms to a multitude of use cases

White papers issued by relevant interest groups, such as [26], indicate that a wide variety of use cases will need to be addressed by future 5G systems. These comprise not only mass market products but also applications for specific (niche) markets with specific requirements. A typical example of the latter is Remote Object Manipulation: Remote Surgery, which requires devices of specific form factors and ultra-high reliability. It is therefore expected that major manufacturers may not be able to provide products suitable for all possible use cases, because of their sheer number. Instead, specialized companies, such as SMEs (Small and Medium Entrepreneurs), will build on generic underlying hardware platforms, which will be parameterized through open source software interfaces and integrated into specialized target form factors. Without open source software interfaces, many of the identified 5G use cases may never be supported.

ii. Enable modification of radio parameters through an evolution of Smartphone apps to RadioApps

The European Commission revised the Radio and Telecommunications Terminal Equipment Directive (R&TTED) and adopted the new Radio Equipment Directive (RED) [27] in 2014. This Directive establishes a regulatory framework in the European Union for making radio equipment available on the market and putting it into service. One of the key novelties introduced by the RED is the possibility of introducing new radio equipment features through software. The concerned RED paragraphs are as follows [27]:

"Article 3 - Essential requirements

3. Radio equipment within certain categories or classes shall be so constructed that it complies with the following essential requirements:

(i) radio equipment supports certain features in order to ensure that software can only be loaded into the radio equipment where the compliance of the combination of the radio equipment and software has been demonstrated."

And

"Article 4 - Provision of information on the compliance of combinations of radio equipment and software

1. Manufacturers of radio equipment and of software allowing radio equipment to be used as intended shall provide the Member States and the Commission with information on the compliance of intended combinations of radio equipment and software with the essential requirements set out in Article 3. Such information shall result from a conformity assessment carried out in accordance with Article 17, and shall be given in the form of a statement of compliance which includes the elements set out in Annex VI. Depending on the specific combinations of radio equipment and software, the information shall precisely identify the radio equipment and the software which have been assessed, and it shall be continuously updated.

2. The Commission shall be empowered to adopt delegated acts in accordance with Article 44 specifying which categories or classes of radio equipment are concerned by the requirement set out in paragraph 1 of this Article.

3. The Commission shall adopt implementing acts laying down the operational rules for making the information on compliance available for the categories and classes specified by the delegated acts adopted pursuant to paragraph 2 of this Article. Those implementing acts shall be adopted in accordance with the examination procedure referred to in Article 45(3)."

In this context, ETSI has developed technical solutions for enabling the reconfiguration of mobile devices through so-called *RadioApps*. Those are similar to existing Smartphone apps, with the difference that the modification of radio parameters is made possible. It should be noted that a substantially different approach to software reconfiguration is taken by ETSI compared to past efforts in the context of Software Defined Radio (SDR). Existing SDR approaches typically rely on a complex computation platform allowing the execution of entire air interfaces or wave forms. Because of the inherent complexity, those solutions have led to poor acceptance in the mass market. The current ETSI approach instead addresses the problem from the other end, building on existing Smartphone apps. It is indeed proposed that an equipment manufacturer can gradually open up its platform to defined internal Application Programming Interfaces (API). Corresponding code is executed in a secure environment called the Radio Virtual Machine (RVM). The platform is thus not fully opened to a third-party software manufacturer but allows access only to clearly identified features. To give a specific example, a manufacturer may choose to provide access to antenna selection APIs to third-party software manufacturers. Then, new RadioApps can be created, providing optimized antenna-selection solutions for a specific context.

The basic system architecture for mobile device reconfiguration is defined in [28] and shown in Figure 4-18.

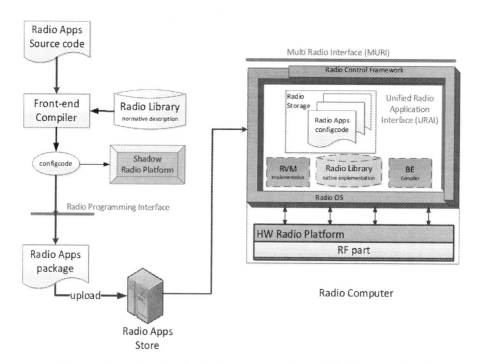

Figure 4-18. *System architecture for Radio Computer, where Radio Library and Back End (BE) compiler are included within the Radio Computer [28]*

ETSI TR 102 967 [29] analyzes requirements related to the issuance of a Declaration of Conformity and its handling in the context of software reconfiguration affecting radio parameters. Such a Declaration of Conformity is required by regulation administrations in Europe before the concerned equipment can be introduced into the single European market.

The ETSI document discusses two potential scenarios for a Declaration of Conformity in the context of a revision of TR 102 967 as of a global application, depending on the applicable legal framework:

Potential Scenario 1: An update of the applicable Declaration of Conformity for the joint operation of Hardware in combination with a new Software Component (RadioApp).

In the European context, it is proposed to build on Radio Equipment Directive, Annex VII: SIMPLIFIED EU DECLARATION OF CONFORMITY;

Initially, the Original Equipment Manufacturer

> *declares that the radio equipment type [designation of type of radio equipment] is in compliance with Directive 2014/53/EU. The full text of the EU declaration of conformity Declaration of Conformity is available at the following internet address:___*

In order to enable joint operation of the available Hardware in combination with a new Software Component (RadioApp), the Declaration of Conformity available at the given Internet Address is updated to include the new configuration.

Potential Scenario 2: Initially, a DoC is issued for available hardware components in combination with Software Components (RadioApps) to be developed in the future.

A future software component is typically made available together with a "Conformity Statement" by the Original Equipment Manufacturer, indicating that the combination of concerned hardware and software complies with the appropriate requirements.

The initial DoC will be not modified, as the Conformity Statement is related to the features enabled by RVM, which limits software components' access to radio parameters as defined by the EN 303 095 concept of "RVM protection classes" [28].

In Scenario 2, the Declaration of Conformity together with the appropriate Conformity Statement is expected to be equivalent to a Scenario 1—the overall responsibility is taken by a single entity, that is, the Original Equipment Manufacturer (OEM), as illustrated in Figure 4-19.

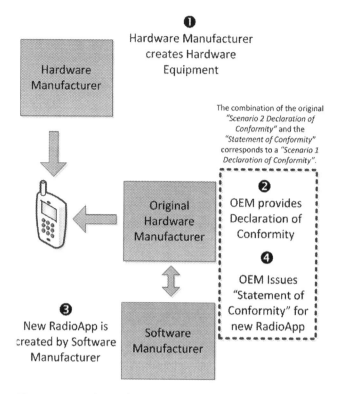

Figure 4-19. *Relationship between Scenario 1 and Scenario 2 declaration of conformity*

These two scenarios for the Declaration of Conformity were presented to the European Telecommunications Conformity Assessment and Market Surveillance Committee (TCAM) in October, 2015. It is expected that regulation issues will be studied further before related products can be introduced into the market.

We've looked here at the European context of software reconfiguration. Other regions may apply different mechanisms, and correspondingly adapted methodologies need to be defined in order to allow the modification of radio parameters through third-party software developers.

Flexible Duplex

Any wireless communication today for 2G, 3G, and 4G wireless communication systems, as well as for wireless connectivity like Bluetooth, WiFi, or WiGig goes simultaneously between transmitter and receiver in both directions and therefore is either a frequency division duplex (FDD) or a time division duplex (TDD) scheme. The duplex scheme is a key element of the system and has to be specified carefully in the system requirements, including performance, efficiency, and power consumption.

In the half-duplex scheme, the terminals comprising a wireless communication link are allowed to transmit only in one direction at a time or in a frequency band. If one terminal is transmitting, the other one must wait until the first terminal stops before transmitting or using another time slot or frequency band for its transmission. In the full duplex scheme, the communicating terminals are allowed to transmit and receive simultaneously, using either different time slots or different frequency bands for their transmission.

In the FDD and TDD duplex schemes, the terminal transmission and reception allocate time and frequency resources orthogonally, creating no interference between transmitter and receiver, with the drawback of requiring resources in time and frequency twice (Figure 4-20). So there is no interference between transmitter and receiver in FDD, because of the separate use of Tx and Rx bands and duplexers.

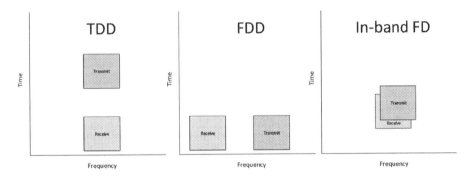

Figure 4-20. *Duplex schemes*

In a flexible duplex scheme, terminals are allowed to transmit within a unified TDD/FDD frame structure and therefore use both modes simultaneously as well. In an in-band full-duplex scheme the terminals transmit and receive simultaneously in the same frequency band, mitigating their self-interference. Since transmission and reception happen at the same time and frequency, the capacity is ideally doubled if we can mitigate the serious self-interference of the leaked Tx signal by more than 110 dB, depending on usage scenario.

One option for this self-interference cancellation is the use of separate transmit and receiver antennas, where one antenna is set locally at null of vertical beam of the other antenna. Disadvantages are the use of at least two antennas, requiring a large space, the very high isolation needed between them, and the loss of channel reciprocity. Another is that transmit beamforming creates a null toward the receiver antenna. Here the drawbacks are the low achievable suppression of less than 30dB, the lack of scalability, the creation of a hole in coverage due to the null, and again the loss of channel reciprocity. Finally, there are open loop approaches using a transmit signal copy and channel estimation of the self-interference channel to make a cancellation signal. Drawbacks here are the extreme accuracy needed for self-interference channel estimation, the impact of radio front-end impairments, and the difficulty of accurately tracking a time-variant channel. So more shared research between radio frequency and signal processing makers is needed to develop commercial products. One example is the closed-loop echo cancellation method implemented purely in the analog domain from Intel, which is robust to phase noise, suffers no performance degradation due to radio frequency impairments in the transmit chain, is applicable to wideband signals, and has no need for additional antennas [31]

The support provided by a highly elastic duplex scheme adapting to the traffic demand and the radio environment will be a key technology for the 5G network architecture, contributing to its flexibility as well to improvements in spectrum efficiency. Increasing spectrum efficiency will require advancing FDD by decreasing or removing guard bands, developing TDD by decreasing guard times, along with effective synchronization and fast switching times, and finally making the application of in-band full-duplex schemes happen. The 5G network architecture needs to be very flexible; in particular it needs to support several kinds of network slicing. For example, networks can be deployed as *frequency divided,* where different frequency bands are assigned to different cell layers using different duplex schemes.

Internet of Things (IoT) and Machine-Type Communications

As outlined in the previous sections, many measures are targeting the mobile broadband evolution. In addition to increased data rates, there is a growing demand for connecting devices or "things" without direct human interaction, the Internet of Things (IoT). When those devices are connected with cellular technology, it is also called Cellular IoT.

Different sets of requirements can be defined for these machine-type communication (MTC) systems. Those requirements span a wide range from massive MTC (M-MTC) to mission-critical MTC (MC-MTC):

M-MTC: connecting a massive amount of devices with typically only infrequent exchange of small amounts of data. Examples are sensor networks or smart meters. Data transfer is delay-tolerant; that is, there's no real-time requirement, and delays of a few seconds or more can be accepted. Because of the massive number of devices, they need to cost well below today's feature phones. Because deployment can include areas with imperfect cellular coverage, like basements or remote rural areas, the coverage provided by today's cellular systems needs to be improved accordingly; a simple measure is to enhance coverage by simple repetition coding. Furthermore, battery lifetime requirements of a couple of years with standard batteries like AA cells may be required for installations at inaccessible locations or simply for cost reasons, as it might be more expensive to regularly exchange batteries than it was to purchase the device. To summarize, M-MTC is characterized by

- Low cost

- Low power

- Enhanced coverage

- Delay tolerance

- Infrequent small data bursts

MC-MTC: connecting devices reliably and with potentially high data rates. Data may be delay-sensitive, as for control of machines or for the *Tactile Internet.* Examples span from industrial control to autonomously driving cars or drone connectivity.

While 5G MTC radio systems are yet to be defined, there are already a couple of activities within 3GPP Release 13 that can set the stage for further evolution, eventually up to 5G.

Within GERAN, an extended coverage EPGRS (EC-EGPRS) system is being defined. EC-EGPRS will extend the coverage of EGPRS by 20 dB toward a maximum coupling loss of 164 dB, where a data rate of 160 bps will still be possible.

Within RAN, there are two parallel Rel-13 activities, FeMTC and NB-IoT:

FeMTC is related to the work item on *"Further LTE Physical Layer Enhancements for MTC"*. It defines a system evolved from LTE with a few simplifications to reduce device complexity: FeMTC operates in 1.4 MHz (6 LTE physical resource blocks), supports only a single antenna at the device, limits peak data rates to 1 Mbps in uplink and downlink by restricting the transport block sizes (TBS) and shall increase the coverage over legacy LTE by 15 dB to a maximum coupling loss of 155.7 dB.

- NB-IoT operates in 200 kHz bandwidth (1 LTE physical resource block) and is comparable with EC-EGPRS in terms of device complexity and coverage. By restricting itself to 200 kHz, it can also replace individual GSM carriers.

Figure 4-21 compares individual LTE-based MTC systems, including Release 8 Cat-1 and Release 12 Cat-0. For power saving, 3GPP defined additional Power Save Mode (PSM) in Release 12 and extended DRX functionality in Release 13, which, of course, can also be supported by the legacy categories, if they support the respective 3GPP release. It will be noted that at the time of writing, Release 13 was not yet finalized.

	Rel. 8 Cat. 1	Rel. 12 Cat. 0	Rel. 13 FeMTC	Rel. 13 NB-IoT
3GPP	Rel. 8+	Rel. 12	Rel. 13	Rel. 13
BW	1.4, 3, 5, 10, 15, 20 MHz	1.4, 3, 5, 10, 15, 20 MHz	1.4 MHz	200 kHz
Number of layers	1	1	1	1
Duplex	Full duplex FDD/ HD-FDD (optional) / TDD	Full duplex FDD / HD-FDD (optional)/TDD	Full duplex FDD / HD-FDD (optional)/TDD	HD-FDD/FDD and TDD
Antenna	Diversity, 2 Rx chains	Single Rx	Single Rx	Single Rx
Peak data rates	10/5 Mbps DL/UL	1 Mbps (limitation in TBS)	1 Mbps	<200 kbps
Max. modulation	64/16-QAM DL/UL 16-QAM	DL 64-QAM / UL16-QAM	DL/UL 16-QAM	DL QPSK/8PSK, UL GMSK/QPSK
Max. UE transmit power	23 dBm	23 dBm	20 dBm (new Power class) and 23 dBm	23 dBm
Power save		PSM	PSM, eDRX	PSM, eDRX
Deployment	Standalone, in LTE channel	Standalone, in LTE channel	Standalone, in LTE channel	Standalone, in LTE channel, in LTE guard bands
Coverage, MCL	DL: 145.4 dB (20 kbps, FDD) UL: 140.7 dB (20 kbps, FDD)	4 dB loss in DL (single Rx)	target 155.7 dB (15 dB improvement)	target 164 dB (160 bps) (20 dB improvement over GPRS)

Figure 4-21. *3GPP MTC radio systems*

References

1. References Samsung Electronics Sets 5G Speed Record at 7.5Gbps, Over 30 Times Faster than 4G LTE. Retrieved from Samsung: `http://www.samsung.com/uk/news/local/samsung-electronics-sets-5g-speed-record-at-7-5gbps-over-30-times-faster-than-4g-lte`, October 2014.
2. Tafazolli, "5G speeds of 1Tbps have been achieved during tests". Retrieved from University of Surrey: `http://www.v3.co.uk/v3-uk/news/2396249/exclusive-university-of-surrey-achieves-5g-speeds-of-1tbps`, Feb 2015
3. R. El Hattachi, J. E. 5G White paper. NGMN, 2015
4. Future Mobile Spectrum Requirements, GSMA Report, 2015
5. ITU-R WP5D. IMT for 2020 and beyond. Retrieved from ITU-R: `http://www.itu.int/en/ITU-R/study-groups/rsg5/rwp5d/imt-2020/Documents/Antipated-Time-Schedule.pdf`
6. RAN 5G Workshop. Retrieved from 3GPP: `http://www.3gpp.org/news-events/3gpp-news/1734-ran_5g`
7. 4G Americas, "2Q2015: LTE Connections Worldwide Double to ¾ Billion", `http://www.4gamericas.org/en/newsroom/press-releases/2q2015-lte-connections-worldwide-double-billion/#sthash.vejcORqu.dpuf`
8. 4G Americas "Recommendations on 5G Requirements and Solutions", White paper, October 2014.
9. Cisco, "Cisco Visual Networking Index: Forecast and Methodology, 2014-2019" White Paper, May 2015.
10. 3GPP, "LTE-Advanced Pro Ready to Go", `http://www.3gpp.org/news-events/3gpp-news/1745-lte-advanced_pro`, October 2015
11. Parkvall, S. Heterogeneous Network Deployments in LTE. Ericsson Review, pp. 34–37.
12. H. Ishii, Y. K. A Novel Architecture for LTE-B. C-plane/U-plane Split and Phantom Cell Concept. GC'12 Workshop: International Workshop on Emerging Technologies for LTE-Advanced and Beyond-4G (pp. 624–630). IEEE.
13. Weiler, R. J at all. Enabling 5G Backhaul and Access with millimeter-waves. IEEE.
14. METIS Project. Retrieved from METIS Project: `https://www.metis2020.com/`
15. METIS II. Retrieved from METIS II: `https://metis-ii.5g-ppp.eu/`
16. S. C. Jha, K. S. Dual Connectivity in LTE Small Cell Networks. Globecom Workshop - Heterogeneous and Small Cell Networks (pp. 1205–1210).
17. H. Peng, T. Y. Extended User/Control Plane Architectures for Tightly Coupled LTE/WiGig Interworking in Millimeter-wave Heterogeneous Networks. IEEE Wireless Communications and Networking Conference (WCNC): - Track 3: Mobile and Wireless Networks (pp. 1548–1553).
18. A. Zakrzewska, D. L.-P. Dual Connectivity in LTE HetNets with Split Control- and User-Plane. Globecom 2013 Workshop - Broadband Wireless Access (pp. 391–396). Atlanta, GA: IEEE.
19. ETSI. Applications and use cases of millimeter wave transmission (ETSI GS mWT 002 V1.1.1). ETSI.
20. al., V. J. Backhaul Requirements for Inter-Site Cooperation in Heterogeneous LTE-Advanced Networks. IEEE ICC (pp. 905–910). IEEE.
21. K. Zhen, L. Z. 10 Gb/s HetSNets with Millimeter-Wave Communications: Access and Networking – Challenges and Protocols. IEEE Communications Magazine, pp. 222–231.
22. 3GPP, "Applications and use cases of millimeter wave transmission", 3GPP 2015
23. Future Mobile Spectrum Requirements, GSMA Report, 2015

24. Management of opportunistic networks through cognitive functionalities, J. Gebert, A. Georgakopoulos, D. Karvounas, V. Stavroulaki, P. Demestichas, 9th Annual Conference on Wireless On-demand Network Systems and Services (WONS), 2012

25. Opportunistic networks for efficient application provisioning in the Future Internet: Business scenarios and technical challenges, A. Georgakopoulos, V. Stavroulaki, J. Gebert, O. Moreno, O. Sallent, M. Matinmikko, M. Filo, D. Boskovic, M. Tosic, M. Mueck, C. Mouton, P. Demestichas, Future Network & Mobile Summit (FutureNetw), 2011

26. NGMN 5G White Paper, Next Generation Mobile Networks Alliance (NGMN), 2015

27. DIRECTIVE 2014/53/EU OF THE EUROPEAN PARLIAMENT AND OF THE COUNCIL of 16 April 2014 on the harmonization of the laws of the Member States relating to the making available on the market of radio equipment and repealing Directive 1999/5/EC

28. ETSI EN 303 095: Reconfigurable Radio Systems (RRS); Radio Reconfiguration related Architecture for Mobile Devices, ETSI, 2015

29. ETSI TR 102 967: Reconfigurable Radio Systems (RRS); Use Cases for dynamic equipment reconfiguration, ETSI, 2015

30. 3GPP, "Mobile-Edge Computing – Introductory", Technical White Paper, Sept 2015

31. Choi, Yang-Seok; Shirani-Mehr, H., "Simultaneous Transmission and Reception: Algorithm, Design and System Level Performance", IEEE Transactions on Wireless Communications, 2013

32. http://www.openstack.org/, Oct. 2015

33. Intel, "Developing High-Performance Flexible SDN & NFV Solutions with Intel Open Network Platform Server Reference Architecture", 2013

CHAPTER 5

Spectrum Sharing

Contributor: Srikathyayani Srikanteswara

As outlined in previous chapters, future fifth-generation (5G) communication systems will increase capacity 1000 to 10,000 times compared to legacy fourth-generation (4G) systems. To achieve that target, the identification of new spectrum for 5G applications is essential. One possibility, of course, relates to the identification of spectrum in higher frequency bands, typically centimeter and millimeter wave bands at 10 GHz and above (as we'll discuss in the next chapter). Still, not all use cases are compatible with wireless propagation conditions in high GHz bands, such as user devices being operated in a highly dynamic and mobile environment. Traditional cellular spectrum below 6 GHz is thus expected to play a key role in the future 5G ecosystem.

Motivation: Spectrum Scarcity and the Need for a New Spectrum Usage Paradigm

Figure 5-1 illustrates the current spectrum allocation in the United States. Traditionally, cellular spectrum has been made available to Mobile Network Operators (MNOs) through suitable repurposing of spectrum. However, this traditional approach is meeting its limits. Below 6 GHz, spectrum is fully allocated to incumbents that fiercely oppose proposals to repurpose "their" spectrum to cellular stakeholders. National Regulation Administrations (NRAs) are clearly under pressure to identify new and novel means for managing spectrum that enables cellular applications to meet their 5G performance targets while satisfying the needs of existing incumbents.

© Intel Corp. 2016
B. Badic et al., *Rolling Out 5G*, DOI 10.1007/978-1-4842-1506-7_5

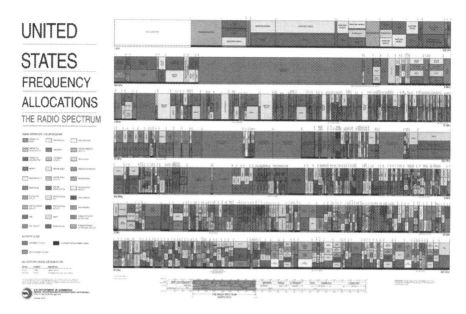

Figure 5-1. *US frequency allocations*

In this context, opportunistic spectrum access in television broadcast bands, described as TV White Spaces (TVWS), has been introduced in the United States [2] and Europe [3]. The basic principle is to allow secondary devices to access spectrum at specific geographic locations and during specific time intervals when the spectrum is not being used by the incumbent (primary user). While TVWS systems sufficiently protect incumbents, there typically is a lack of efficient Quality-of-Service (QoS) management mechanism between secondary systems themselves. Furthermore, the actual availability of TVWS spectrum is uncertain, in particular in densely populated areas. These issues have ultimately hindered the commercial success of TVWS technology.

With the lessons learned from the TVWS system definition, deployment, and operation, a second-generation spectrum sharing technology is being developed in Europe and the US with the objective to eventually provide global coverage in applicable bands. The European Telecommunications Standards Institute (ETSI) and the Conférence Européenne des Administrations des Postes et des Télécommunications (CEPT) have developed a number of documents enabling the usage of the Licensed Shared Access (LSA) scheme in Europe in the 2.3–2.4 GHz LTE band 40 (a Time Division Duplex (TDD) band) [4]. The Federal Communications Commission (FCC) issued a Report and Order related to the operation of the Spectrum Access System (SAS) in the United States in the frequency band 3.55–3.7 GHz (LTE TDD bands 42 and 43) [5]. These systems are expected to provide a key component for future-generation spectrum management. The following sections provide an overview and analysis of both systems.

Overview of Licensed Shared Access (LSA) and Spectrum Access System (SAS) Spectrum Sharing

We'll begin our overview of the two primary spectrum-sharing technologies with a look at the use cases they are being designed for, and then outline their respective architectures.

Key Use Cases

The main use case for LSA technology is as follows: a 3GPP LTE network is operated on a licensed shared basis in the 2.3–2.4 GHz frequency band, which corresponds to 3GPP LTE band 40. It is expected that LTE MNOs will engage in multiple-year sharing contracts with incumbents (such as military stakeholders, professional video camera services, and others), typically for 10 years or more. This long-term certainty is a key requirement for justifying large-scale investments in cellular network infrastructure. Still, the incumbent (tier-1) user is prioritized over the licensee (tier-2); that is, the concerned MNO is required to vacate the LSA band for the given geographic area, frequency range, and period of time for which the incumbent requires access to the resource. Detailed conditions are negotiated between the two parties in the sharing agreement.

Typically, the LSA band is combined with LTE operation in a dedicated licensed spectrum through suitable Carrier Aggregation (CA) mechanisms. Because legacy LTE systems in Europe are mainly based on Frequency Division Duplex (FDD) technology, the 3GPP Release-12 FDD/TDD CA feature is required for a suitable combination of existing deployment with LTE LSA modes. Figure 5-2 illustrates the basic principle.

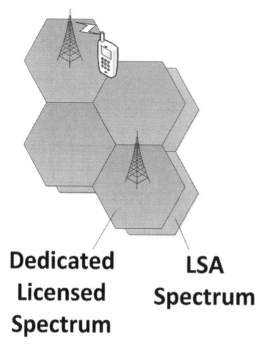

Dedicated Licensed Spectrum

LSA Spectrum

Figure 5-2. *LSA-based spectrum sharing*

The main use case for SAS Technology is similar to the LSA case: A 3GPP LTE network is operated on a licensed shared basis in the 3.55–3.7 GHz frequency band, which corresponds to 3GPP LTE TDD bands 42 and 43. A major difference from LSA consists in the fact that licensed spectrum slots are only available in parts of the SAS band (up to 70 MHz) for Priority Access License (PAL) tier-2 users. The remaining part of the spectrum, along with unused portions of the PAL slots, is available to a new user class, called General Authorized Access (GAA) tier-3 users (the "use-it-or-share-it" rule). This tier-3 class does not exist in the LSA system definition. GAA users may typically operate LTE License Assisted Access (LAA) or WiFi type systems, including modifications required for adaptation to the SAS requirements imposed by the FCC [5].

It should be noted that both systems, LSA and SAS, are defined for use in a specific frequency band. The basic operational principles of those systems, however, are frequency-agnostic and can be applied straightforwardly to other bands. NRAs will be able to utilize the technologies as a new tool in the frequency management toolbox to allocate suitable bandwidth to wireless broadband systems.

System Architecture

The basic system architecture is shown in Figure 5-3 for LSA and in Figure 5-4 for SAS.

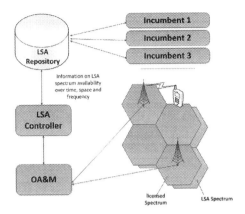

Figure 5-3. *Licensed Shared Access (LSA) architecture*

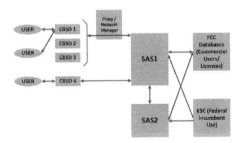

Figure 5-4. *Spectrum Access System (SAS) architecture*

Figure 5-3 illustrates the LSA system architecture as defined in ETSI TS 103 235 [7]. In this context, spectrum management mainly relies on a centralized database known as the LSA Repository. Incumbents are required to provide a-priori usage information to the database on the availability of LSA spectrum over geographic space and time. Depending on this information, the LTE system is granted access or requested to vacate concerned bands through the control mechanisms within the LSA Controller. In this operational approach, no sensing mechanisms are required to support the system for the identification of incumbent operation.

Figure 5-4 illustrates the SAS architecture. A main difference from LSA lies in the fact that SAS is designed to ensure coexistence with incumbent users who are not able to provide any a-priori information to a central database. In the context of SAS, the incumbents include military services using networks operated mainly close to US coastal areas. For this reason, an Environmental Sensing Capability (ESC) component is added, which performs required sensing tasks. The spectrum access decisions for tier-3 and tier-2 users are finally based on these sensing results.

LSA and Relevant Incumbents

The LSA system will address the needs of the following stakeholders:

> Incumbent Users; that is, primary users who may sublicense spectrum to LSA licensees under certain conditions

> LSA Licensees operating a wireless system under a sharing agreement, typically MNOs providing 3GPP LTE services

> NRAs, which will be able to monitor spectrum sharing activities

Note that these guidelines imply a substantial change over, for example, TVWS communication systems. The LSA scheme in particular provides a clear business case in which a rental relationship between incumbents and LSA licensees leads to a defined money flow, with LSA licensees obtaining guaranteed Quality-of-Service (QoS) conditions in a given geographic area, frequency band, and time period. TVWS neither offer such a clear business model for all stakeholders nor a guaranteed level of QoS, which may at least partly explain the technology's limited commercial success.

System Design

In Europe, the 2.3–2.4 GHz band has been identified for an initial deployment of LSA [4]. This band has been defined as LTE TDD band 40 and is used in other regions as dedicated licensed LTE spectrum. ETSI's Reconfigurable Radio Systems (RRS) Technical Committee has developed corresponding System Requirements [6] and System Architecture [7] solutions, defining the key building blocks and interfaces for the framework just described as illustrated in Figure 5-5.

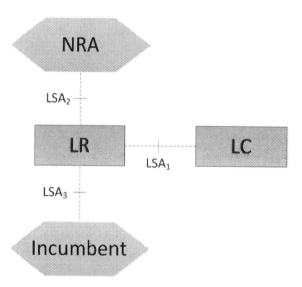

Figure 5-5. *LSA architecture reference model*

The LSA Repository (LR) represents an entity providing database and other functions as described in the following paragraphs. In the European LSA context, the LSA Repository plays a key role, as all information related to spectrum occupancy is provided by the Incumbent to the database. The LSA Controller (LC) introduces processing and decision-making capabilities, building on the data elements provided by the LSA Repository. The LSA Controller will interact with an MNO's Operations, Administration, and Management (OA&M) framework to indicate spectrum availability, request short-term vacating of the spectrum, and similar tasks, as illustrated in Figure 5-5. The US model follows a different strategy; all such information needs to be derived by an Environmental Sensing Capability (ESC) and must comply with strict confidentiality requirements as described in the following sections.

In accordance with the definitions in [7], a more detailed explanation of the LSA Repository and LSA Controller components is shown in Figure 5-6.

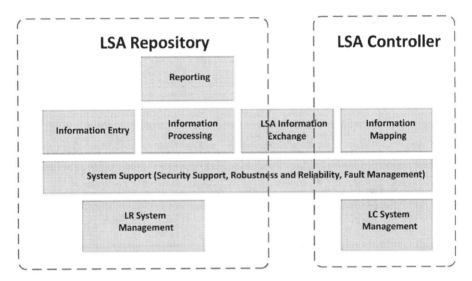

Figure 5-6. *Mapping of high level functions and function groups to logical elements*

The high-level functions introduced in Figure 5-6 are derived from the ETSI requirements document [6] and are further detailed in the following list.

- The Information Entry function enables the entry and storage of information that is required for the operation of the LSA system; it comprises in particular the following: i) information about the Sharing Framework between Incumbent(s) and LSA Licensee(s) indicating mutually agreed sharing conditions for the concerned band(s), ii) LSA Licensee information, such as its identity, and iii) information about the Incumbent's LSA spectrum resource usage, protection requirements, and so on.

- The Information Processing function supports the derivation of information about LSA spectrum resource availability for each Licensee, to be provided to the Information Exchange function for forwarding to the respective Information Mapping function of the LSA Licensee. This function uses data provided through the Information Entry function. It also includes support for multiple Incumbents and multiple LSA Licensees, scheduled and on-demand modes of operation, and logging of processing information.

- The Information Mapping function receives LSA spectrum resource availability information, confirms reception, and initiates respective operations in the MFCN. It also provides acknowledgement to the Information Exchange function (for forwarding to the Information Processing function) when changes in the MFCN are processed.

- The Reporting function is responsible for creating and providing reports about the LSA System operation to the Administration/NRA, Incumbent(s), and/or LSA Licensee(s) on an on-demand or scheduled basis.

- The LSA Information Exchange function supports communication mechanisms, internal to the LSA system, for exchanging LSA spectrum resource availability information and related acknowledgements.

- The System Support Functions Group comprises the following: i) a Security Support function for support of authentication and authorization as well as services to support integrity and confidentiality of data; ii) a Robustness and Reliability function for support of mechanisms to maintain robustness and reliability against failures and malicious attacks; and iii) a Fault Management function for support of failure detection in the LSA system, along with subsequent generation and delivery of respective failure notification(s) to LSA Licensee(s) and Incumbent(s) and initiation of respective operations in the LSA system.

- The System Management functions group comprises the following: i) Operation, administration, and maintenance tasks in the LSA System; ii) Identity management (comprising user identity and authentication management, and user authorization profiles); and iii) System management, which is separate for LSA Repository and LSA Controller, since these logical entities belong to different operation domains.

It is expected that the system approach just described is able to satisfy the needs of all stakeholders, including Incumbents, LSA Licensees, NRAs and others such that i) the Incumbent will be able to monetize underused spectrum, ii) the LSA Licensee will be able to access additional spectrum, enjoying guaranteed QoS conditions, and iii) the NRAs ensure the best possible usage of already allocated spectrum.

Standards and Regulation Framework

Activities related to LSA and SAS are currently ongoing in the ETSI Reconfigurable
Radio Systems (RRS) Technical Committee with a focus on LSA, in the Wireless
Innovation Forum (WInnF) with a focus on SAS, and in 3GPP targeting a global solution
encompassing LSA and SAS.

The ETSI work has produced documents [4], [6], and [7] and will continue its activity
with a focus on defining stage-3 interfaces that are outside the 3GPP system, such as the
definition of the LSA1 Interface as illustrated in Figure 5-5 earlier.

3GPP is discussing the integration and linkage of the LSA and SAS components into
the 3GPP architecture. Document [8] proposes one possible way to include the LSA and
3GPP sides under a common umbrella, as illustrated in Figure 5-7.

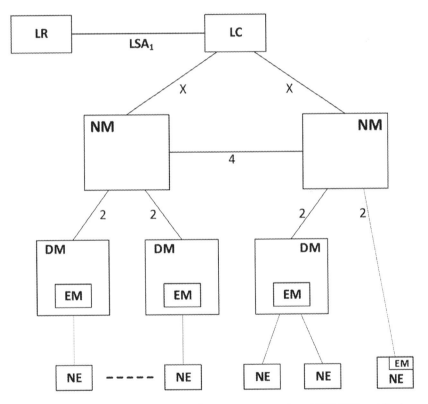

Figure 5-7. *Integration and linkage of LSA components into 3GPP SAS architecture*

As defined in [19], the corresponding entities in Figure 5-7 provide the following functionalities:

- A Network Manager (NM) provides a package of end-user functions for the management of a network, mainly as supported by the EM(s), but it may also involve direct access to the Network Elements (NEs). All communication with the network is based on open and well-standardized interfaces that support management of multivendor and multitechnology Network Elements.

- A Domain Manager (DM) provides element management and domain management functions for a subnetwork. Interworking domain managers provide multivendor and multitechnology network management functions.

- An Element Manager (EM) provides a package of end-user functions for management of a set of closely related types of network elements. These functions can be divided into two main categories: Element Management and Subnetwork Management functions.

- A Network Element (NE) corresponds to a discrete telecommunication entity, which can be managed over a specific interface, such as the RNC.

The WInnF leverages its long-term relationship with the US Department of Defense (DoD) to define an SAS system approach that is compatible with the needs of the US incumbents, which are mainly Naval shipborne radar and satellite services. Protection of satellite services is a key aspect of the FCC's second further notice of proposed rulemaking [5].

From the regulatory perspective, the European CEPT organization has acted following earlier investigations and in answer to a corresponding mandate by the European Commission [9–11]. CEPT has produced a number of Reports, Recommendations, and Decisions [12–16] and has finally closed the corresponding working groups. From a CEPT perspective, the work is achieved and the actual usage of the LSA band in Europe now depends on the respective NRAs to enable the usage of spectrum sharing on the national territory.

Protection of Incumbents and Neighboring Licensees

The current usage of the 2.3–2.4 GHz LSA band varies over the European nations. While professional video camera services represent the main incumbents for some countries, others have allocated the spectrum also to military aircraft telemetry services, amateur radio, police wireless communication, and so on. Detailed information for each country is available in the ECO Frequency Information System [18]. Based on where corresponding incumbent systems are operated and which level of protection they require, the maximum LSA output power levels can be derived as shown in Figure 5-8, which illustrates France as an example.

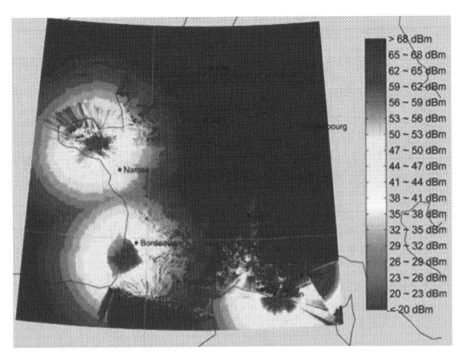

Figure 5-8. *LSA spectrum availability in France [17]*

Traditionally, incumbent systems are protected by exclusion zones, which prohibit the use of interfering equipment within a given geographic zone. It turns out that the corresponding zones need to be of considerable size to sufficiently protect the incumbents, since the interfering system can operate without restrictions starting from the boundaries of the exclusion zone. To maximize the geographic area in which the operation of LSA is possible, ETSI RRS has identified further zone types, which make it possible to reduce the constraints on the LSA system [6]:

- Exclusion Zone: A geographical area within which LSA Licensees are not allowed to have active radio transmitters. An exclusion zone is normally applicable for a defined frequency range and time period.

- Restriction Zone: A geographical area within which LSA Licensees are allowed to operate radio transmitters, under certain restrictive conditions (for example, maximum EIRP limits and/or constraints on antenna parameters). A restriction zone is normally applicable for a defined frequency range and time period.

- Protection Zone: A geographical area within which Incumbent receivers will not be subject to harmful interference caused by LSA Licensees' transmissions. A protection zone is defined using specific measurement quantities and thresholds (such as a mean field strength that does not exceed a defined value in dBµV/m/MHz at a defined receiver antenna height above ground level). A protection zone is normally applicable for a defined frequency range and time period.

Concerning requirements for protection of neighboring LSA systems operated by distinct MNOs, it is mainly cross-border issues that need to be considered for efficient operation close to national borders. Note that LSA does not require complex interference mitigation across small geographic areas with different licensing situations; it is assumed that an LSA license is allocated to an MNO (or other LSA Licensee) across an entire country or at least for a large geographic area. This is in contrast to the FCC SAS concept, where interference mitigation is required between neighboring census tracts, which may be of small geographic size in densely populated areas.

Intra-MNO-System Interference Mitigation through LSA

Future 5G network deployments will provide increased energy efficiency and spatial utilization of the licensed spectrum, but such a diverse and heterogeneous cell deployment will create some important technical challenges that need to be overcome first. One of the critical aspects in such dense heterogeneous networks is rich and uncoordinated inter-cell interference within the system of a given MNO. LSA is expected to provide a new tool to address at least some of the interference cases.

While LSA spectrum can be used straightforwardly as additional spectrum for voice and data communication, the available LSA spectrum can be also exploited for Inter-Cell Interference Coordination (ICIC). Because LSA provides additional spectral resources over a given geographic area, for a given time interval and a given frequency band, depending on interference levels and the need for interference mitigation, a trade-off can be made between LSA resources assigned for voice and data and those assigned for ICIC. Introducing collaborative spectrum sensing and more flexibility in spectrum sharing, the licensed users can dynamically access and share spectrum without causing interference to primary users. By intelligently allocating LSA spectrum to both central and cell-edge cells in a network, interference can be reduced significantly and implementation of complex and high-cost interference mitigation techniques in the UE receiver chain can be avoided.

Challenges and Next Steps for LSA

The regulations related to LSA have been defined by CEPT, and the corresponding work is complete. The standards work is in an advanced stage in ETSI, while 3GPP will provide a first solution in its Release 13. The technology is likely to evolve further in Release 14 and beyond. The main challenge relates to the willingness of NRAs to finally enable the usage of the target 2.3–2.4 GHz band in their respective nations. Corresponding trials are in preparation in France and Italy; further countries are expected to follow. Once LSA has been proven to operate efficiently, the obvious next step is to identify further target bands and to adapt the LSA scheme to inherent requirements (for example, support of higher dynamicity). It is expected that LSA will become a key tool in the regulation toolbox, providing spectrum resources for 5G systems and beyond to meet the expected thousand-fold to ten-thousand-fold capacity requirements.

SAS and Relevant Incumbents

Following an NOI (Notice of Inquiry) and an NPRM (Notice of Proposed Rulemaking), the FCC formally released the Report and Order (R&O) to the Citizen's Broadband Radio Service (CBRS) 3.5 GHz band in April, 2015. The FCC outlines a three-priority access system for sharing the band with its incumbents. It requires protection of incumbent military radar and fixed satellite services. The three tiers of the band are: Incumbent (tier-1), Priority Access (PA, tier-2), and General Authorized Access (GAA, tier-3), as described next. Note that LSA is based on a two-tier model, while SAS introduces three levels of priority.

1. Incumbents: They are the current users of the spectrum. They can use the spectrum they have been heretofore using, without any limitations. The main incumbent is the DoD with naval shipborne radars. Other incumbents include Fixed Satellite Systems (FSS), Radio Location Services (RLS), and Terrestrial Wireless systems. The incumbents get interference protection from the lower two tiers.

2. Priority Access (PA): This is similar to a licensed spectrum that can be won in an auction. However, PA Licensees (PALs) must vacate the spectrum for an incumbent should they need to use it. Priority Access operations receive protection from GAA operations. Priority Access Licenses (PALs), defined as an authorization to use a 10 MHz channel in a single census tract for three years, will be assigned in up to 70 MHz of the 3550–3650 MHz portion of the band [5]. Currently there are over 74,000 census tracts, with a targeted population of 4000 in the United States. Note, however, that the frequencies themselves are not necessarily fixed. In other words, if a carrier wins 1×10 MHz channel, then it is guaranteed 10 MHz of licensed spectrum (provided there is no incumbent) in the 3.5 GHz band, but the actual channel is not fixed. However, the FCC also indicates that the frequency will remain as static as possible. The suggested users include carriers, smart grid, rural broadband, small-cell backhaul, and other point-to-multipoint networks. The PALs get interference protection from the tier below them but not from incumbents.

3. General Authorized Access (GAA): This level of access is allowed throughout the 3.55–3.7 GHz band but get no interference protection from other CBRS users (PA and incumbent). GAA users are guaranteed at least 80 MHz of spectrum.

The deployment of systems is divided into two phases; the first phase uses the SAS to coordinate spectrum access outside the exclusion zones. In phase two, the ESC coordinates transmissions inside the exclusion zones. The ESC is expected to be a form of sensor network.

The FCC outlines the high-level SAS architecture in the R&O as shown in Figure 5-9.

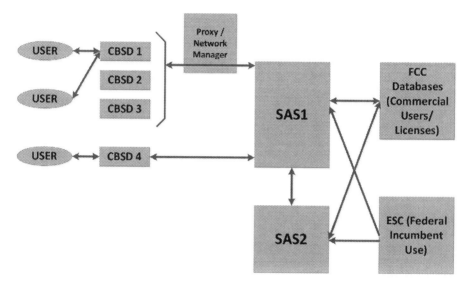

Figure 5-9. *FCC's SAS architecture*

The main functions of the SAS include incumbent protection and protection of PALs from GAA. To perform these functions, the FCC outlines a set of rules where the Citizens Broadband Radio Service Devices (CBSDs) must register with the SAS, giving it their location and other details. The SAS then allocates channels that PA and GAA users can access. The SAS can also limit the maximum power of CBSDs to perform interference mitigation between tiers. The end user terminals wait for authorization from the corresponding CBSD before transmitting in the band. All devices must be able to transmit and receive in the entire 3.5 GHz band even if they are not deployed in that manner. Comparing SAS and LSA, the SAS entity can be considered the counterpart of the LSA Controller. However, ETSI defined in ETSI TS 103 235 [7] that this entity must be within the MNO network. In SAS, the interference coordination across multiple networks is expected to require an SAS entity that is at least partly located outside a specific MNO's network domain.

The FCC defines three types of devices: Category A, with a maximum EIRP of 30 dBm/10 MHz; a slightly higher-power Category B (non-rural) with an EIRP of 40 dBm/10 MHz; and Category C, with an EIRP of 47 dBm/10 MHz.

The emission mask is specified as shown in Figure 5-10, where the Out Of Band (OOB) emissions are limited to -13 dBm at the adjacent channel and -25 dBm at the alternate adjacent channel. There is a special requirement of -40 dBm (20 MHz away) at the two edges of the 3.5 GHz band.

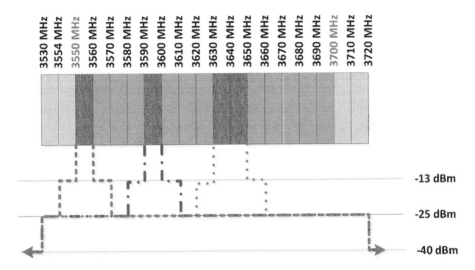

Figure 5-10. *3.5 GHz emission mask*

SAS Differences from LSA

The LSA system is based on two tiers, which each get exclusive access to the spectrum while they are using it. Further, the incumbent populates a database indicating when the secondary user can access the spectrum. By contrast, the 3.5 GHz spectrum has three tiers, with a tier-3 component that closely relates to unlicensed operation and does not exist in the LSA system. However the most notable difference is probably the fact that the DoD will not populate any databases with usage information; it has to be entirely determined by sensing. This puts accurate and reliable sensing technologies in the forefront; with LSA, by contrast, those technologies could be used to improve network performance but are not essential for accessing the band.

The interference mitigation problem is also exacerbated in the 3.5 GHz system for two reasons. First, census tracts are based on population and not area. As a result, in densely populated urban areas, they can be as small as a few blocks, which greatly increases the coordination needed for interference mitigation along each of these boundaries. Second, the GAA users need to be actively managed to prevent interference with the PAL users; something that is not needed in LSA.

The following tables summarize some of the key differences and similarities of both systems. Table 5-1 focuses on use cases and Table 5-2 on technical parameters and configurations.

Table 5-1. *Comparison of Use Cases for Spectrum Sharing*

Use Case	Availability in Europe (LSA)	Avalability in the US (SAS)
Provide capacity extension to carriers on co-primary basis (quasi-licensed)	✔	✔
Enable new business cases, such as local businesses owning spectrum in a small geographic area	✘	✔
Enable license-by-rule usage of spectrum, for tasks like cellular off-loading	✘	✔

Table 5-2. *Functional Overview of Spectrum Sharing*

Parameter	Configuration in Europe (LSA)	Configuration in the US (SAS)
Frequency Band	2.3–2.4 GHz (LTE Band 40)	3.55–3.7 GHz (LTE Bands 42/3)
Usage Tiers	1st tier: Incumbent User 2nd tier: (Co-primary) Licensee	1st tier: Incumbent User 2nd tier: Primary Access Licensee 3rd tier: General Authorized Access
Incumbent Protection	Incumbent protection through database	Sensing-based protection of incumbents
Interference Mitigation	Not required	Interference mitigation across census tracts
Protection of Licensee Information Assets	Full protection	Interference mitigation requires licensee's configuration data
Licensing Period	To be negotiated (target: >10 yrs)	3 yrs (first license: 6 yrs)

Standardization and System Design

The FCC has defined the high-level functionalities of the SAS system (the SAS entity coordinates and authorizes access across users) and the ESC that is needed for transmitting inside the exclusion zone. The Wireless Innovation Forum (WInnForum) is currently developing corresponding specifications with the support of its members from industry (equipment and device manufacturers, and service providers) and DoD. A possible approach for SAS architecture and interface definitions is shown in Figure 5-11.

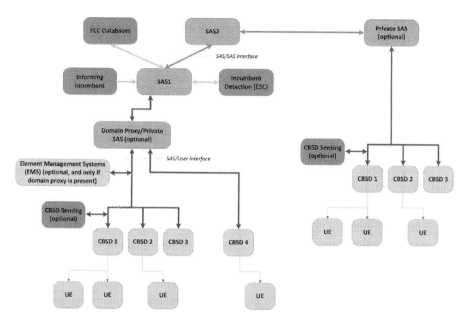

Figure 5-11. *SAS system and interfaces*

The SAS needs to interface with other SASes, with the ESC, and with the FCC's databases. Additionally, there could be incumbents willing to report their band usage either directly to the SAS or via a database that would be hosted by the SAS. There are also interfaces with the CBSDs that are registered to it. Additionally, there could be special types of SAS that serve the needs of the service provider but that have to interface with other SASes for interference protection and incumbent protection.

Protection of Incumbents and Neighboring Users

Similar to LSA, the SAS system needs to protect incumbent systems. Furthermore, as mentioned previously, the FCC introduces a spectrum-auctioning mechanism based on census tracts, which requires mutual protection of PAL and GAA users across neighboring census tracts. The latter aspect is not considered in LSA, since it is assumed that a given LSA spectrum block is licensed to a given LSA Licensee across an entire regulation domain (meeting the requirements of Exclusion, Restriction, and Protection Zones).

Protection of Incumbents

The 3500 MHz band is critical to DoD radar operations and other systems, as it offers a specific propagation and atmospheric condition that is unique to this frequency range. In this region of the spectrum, multipath propagation problems decrease, which is critical to for radar systems for the detection of targets at low elevation angles.

Highpowered defense radar systems are operated on fixed, mobile, shipborne, and airborne platforms. Radar systems are used for radiolocation and radio navigation services. Among these are

- Fleet air defense

- Missile and gunfire control

- Bomb scoring

- Battlefield weapon location

- Air traffic control (ATC), including

  - Radio navigation services, including air operations, ATC, and approach control

  - The ATC also serves as backup for shortrange, air-search radar systems. The Navy shipborne radars operate on 21 frequencies or channels throughout this band.

- Range detection

More specifically, in the 3.55–3.65 GHz band Radiolocation Services (RLS) are operated with priority on military RLS operations (DoD radar systems) as well as ground-based Aeronautical Radio Navigation Systems (ARNS). In 3.6–3.65 GHz, the spectrum is used by Fixed Satellite Systems (FSS), Space-to-Earth, for finite time. 3.65–3.7 GHz is currently exploited for Fixed Satellite and grandfathered terrestrial wireless systems, federal RLS, and ship stations (44nm off shore).

In 2010, the NTIA recommended that the 3.55–3.65 GHz bands can be made available for wireless broadband, with some geographic limitations. Staying above 3.55 GHz greatly reduces the potential for interference from high-power radar operating below 3.5 GHz. As already noted, service rules based on license exclusion/protection zones have to be implemented along the US coastline to protect base stations from high-power US Navy radar systems (see Figure 5-12).

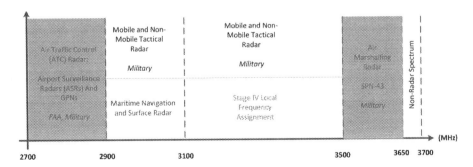

Figure 5-12. *S-band radar*

While the Exclusion/Protection Zones originally proposed by NTIA covered approximately 60 percent of the US population, those zones have recently been reduced by 77 percent [20]. In its current form, they are expected to exclude about 40 percent of the US population in the first phase of SAS deployment; that is, without the usage of the ESC dedicated to spectrum sensing. Once suitable ESC technology is available and certified by the FCC, SAS PAL and GAA systems will be able to operate also within Exclusion/Protection Zones (Figure 5-13), while ensuring sufficient protection of the incumbent(s).

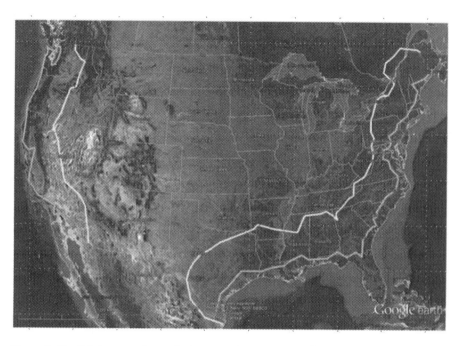

Figure 5-13. *Shipborne radar-exclusion zone, lower 48 states (yellow line = fast track exclusion zone, blue line = revised exclusion zone) [20]*

In addition to shipborne radar systems, ground-based radar systems are operated at locations within the United States. Only a small number of sites require protection exclusion zones, since the use of the upper portion of the tuning range of these radar systems is not required. The radio frequency filter has to provide 30 to 40 dB of attenuation at 3.5 GHz to mitigate the potential of high-power interference effects. See Figure 5-14 for an example.

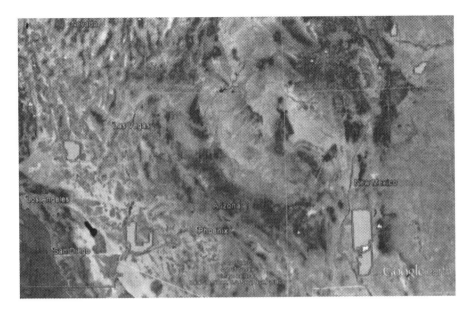

Figure 5-14. *Ground-based radar exclusion zones, middle west coast [20]*

Protection of Neighboring Users

PALs are assigned for 10 MHz unpaired channels in a single census tract. Census tracts vary in size depending on the population density of the region, with tracts as small as one square mile or less in dense urban areas and up to 85,000 square miles in sparsely populated rural regions. Note that this allocation is substantially different from the LSA case, where a given frequency block is allocated to a single given LSA Licensee across an entire regulation domain, typically an entire country.

A snapshot of the allocation of census tracts in New York City is illustrated in Figure 5-15. Since PAL and GAA allocations may differ between neighboring census tracts, the use of SAS implies the requirement for a complex interference mitigation solution. Indeed, PAL and GAA users are required to interact with SAS entities and to share required information so that sufficient levels of interference mitigation can be achieved.

Figure 5-15. Census tracts in New York City [21]

Challenges and Next Steps for SAS

The three-tier model is a completely new concept in regulations. Service providers are accustomed to the certainty that exclusive licenses provide. A key challenge will be to ensure that industry and ecosystem come together and are able to deploy this band. For the band to be viable to service providers as a PAL channel, the regulations need to ensure that there is some guarantee for renewing the spectrum licenses. Further, the concept of SAS needs to be developed very carefully to ensure that the needs of the incumbents as well as the commercial users are met. The incumbents' main concerns include interference protection, privacy, and security of DoD related data, like ship locations and activity details. On the other hand, confidentiality of the network information is equally important to the service providers. Designing the ESC and SAS to accommodate the needs of the ecosystem players will ensure success in the band.

Furthermore, as mention in the section "Intra-MNO-System Interference Mitigation through LSA" for the LSA case, intra-system interference mitigation is expected to be a key challenge in future wireless networks. While SAS can address this challenge in a way similar to LSA, the interference situation is more complex in the case of SAS deployment: unlike LSA, SAS needs to consider interference originating from distinct MNOs with networks being deployed in neighboring census tracts. Because there is typically no coordination between distinct MNOs, it is difficult to deploy any conventional interference mitigation technique. Therefore, novel and disruptive approaches and techniques will be needed to reduce interference between two MNOs while limiting the exchange of information between the two to a strict minimum.

Challenges and Next Steps for the Evolution of LSA and SAS

The introduction of LSA and SAS marks a substantial change in spectrum management by NRAs. It is a de facto confirmation that traditional refarming approaches are reaching their limits and cannot guarantee the availability of broadband wireless bandwidth as required for future 5G communication systems and beyond. It will take time until all stakeholders accept this fact and finally rely on shared spectrum as a key ingredient to their network.

Furthermore, there are two distinct technologies on the table—LSA and SAS— which should ideally converge into a single framework to guarantee rapid adoption and deployment. 3GPP has recently begun to consider spectrum sharing in a study item [22] that targets a worldwide solution. It remains to be seen whether a harmonized solution that covers the current European and US approaches—and possibly includes specific flavors required for Asia and other markets—can finally be agreed upon.

While spectrum sharing represents one way forward for providing additional capacity for future broadband wireless systems, its future success will certainly depend on the level of adoption of alternative approaches. Among the latter, the usage of higher frequency bands, including mmWave spectrum up to 70 GHz and beyond, is currently considered to be promising. However, the suitability of mmWave technology to mobile use cases is currently under study, and its sustainability needs to be proven. The final success and feasibility of such alternative technologies will substantially impact the need for and adoption of spectrum sharing below 6 GHz, and potentially the application of solutions like LSA and SAS in even higher frequency bands [23].

References

1. United States Frequency Allocations, U.S. DEPARTMENT OF COMMERCE, National Telecommunications and Information Administration, Office of Spectrum Management

2. Overview of FCC's New Rules for TV White Space Devices and database updates, Allen Yang (FCC, USA), ITU-R SG 1/WP 1B WORKSHOP: SPECTRUM MANAGEMENT ISSUES ON THE USE OF WHITE SPACES BY COGNITIVE RADIO SYSTEMS, Geneva, 20 January 2014

3. ETSI EN 301 598 V1.0.0: White Space Devices (WSD); Wireless Access Systems operating in the 470 MHz to 790 MHz frequency band; Harmonized EN covering the essential requirements of Article 3.2 of the R&TTE Directive, April 2014

4. ETSI TR 103 113 V1.1.1: Electromagnetic compatibility and Radio spectrum Matters (ERM); System Reference document (SRdoc); Mobile broadband services in the 2 300 MHz–2 400 MHz frequency band under Licensed Shared Access regime, July 2013

5. REPORT AND ORDER AND SECOND FURTHER NOTICE OF PROPOSED RULEMAKING, FCC 15-47, Adopted: April 17, 2015 Released: April 21, 2015

6. ETSI TS 103 154 V1.1.1: Reconfigurable Radio Systems (RRS); System requirements for operation of Mobile Broadband Systems in the 2300 MHz–2400 MHz band under Licensed Shared Access (LSA), October 2014

7. ETSI TS 103 235 V1.1.1: Reconfigurable Radio Systems (RRS); System Architecture and High Level Procedures for operation of Licensed Shared Access (LSA) in the 2300 MHz–2400 MHz band, 2015

8. LSA management architecture", INTEL contribution, 3GPP TSG SA WG5 (Telecom Management) Meeting #102, 24 - 28 August, 2015, Beijing, China

9. Report on CUS and other spectrum sharing approaches, RSPG (Radio Spectrum Policy Group), RSPG11-392, 2011

10. RSPG Opinion on Licensed Shared Access, RSPG (Radio Spectrum Policy Group), RSPG13-538, 2013

11. European Commission (EC) mandate to CEPT for the 2300–2400 MHz frequency band in the EU issued in March 2014

12. ECC Report 205: Licensed Shared Access (LSA), Feb. 2014

13. ECC Recommendation ECC/REC/(14)04 on "Cross-border coordination for MFCN and between MFCN and other systems in the frequency band 2300-2400 MHz", May 2014

14. ECC Decision ECC/DEC/(14)02 on "Harmonized conditions for MFCN in the 2300-2400 MHz band", June 2014

15. ECC Report 55: Report A from CEPT to the European Commission in response to the Mandate on 'Harmonized technical conditions for the 2300–2400 MHz ('2.3 GHz') frequency band in the EU for the provision of wireless broadband electronic communications services; Technical conditions for wireless broadband usage of the 2300–2400 MHz frequency band, CEPT, November 2014

16. ECC Report 56: Report B1 from CEPT to the European Commission in response to the Mandate on 'Harmonized technical conditions for the 23002400 MHz ('2.3 GHz') frequency band in the EU for the provision of wireless broadband electronic communications services; Technological and regulatory options facilitating sharing between Wireless broadband applications (WBB) and the relevant incumbent service/application in the 2.3 GHz band, 2015

17. Spectrum Availability Simulation Environment, RED Technologies, France, 2015

18. ECO Frequency Information System, http://www.efis.dk/

19. 3GPP TS 32.101 (V11.2.0), Technical Specification 3rd Generation Partnership Project; Technical Specification Group Services and System Aspects; Telecommunication management; Principles and high level requirements (Release 11)

20. 3.5 GHz Exclusion Zone Analyses and Methodology, 500 MHz Initiative Spectrum Engineering Spectrum Management 3550-3650 MHz, NTIA Technical Report TR-15-517, June 18, 2015

21. United States Census Bureau, Geographic Terms and Concepts—Census Tract, available at: http://www.census.gov/geo/reference/gtc/gtc_ct.html (last visited September 5, 2013); Some information Calculated using Geolytics Population estimates 2012 from US Geography obtained from United States Census Bureau, Tiger/Line Shapefiles and Tiger/Line Files, available at: https://www.census.gov/geo/maps-data/data/tiger-line.html (Last visited September 5, 2013).

22. 3GPP TR 32.855, Technical Report, 3rd Generation Partnership Project; Technical Specification Group Services and System Aspects; Telecommunication management; Study on OAM support for Licensed Shared Access (LSA); (Release 13), 2015

23. Licensed shared access for wave cellular broadband communications; Markus Mueck, Ingolf Karls, Reza Arefi, Thomas Haustein, Wilhelm Keusgen; 1st International Workshop on Cognitive Cellular Systems (CCS), 2014

CHAPTER 6

■ ■ ■

The Disruptor: The Millimeter Wave Spectrum

Contributor: Alexander Maltsev

The fast development of smart and connected products, including consumer electronics, means that for the best user experience, wireless networks need to operate in frequency bands both below and above 6 GHz. The millimeter wave spectrum, as noted in previous chapters, is mainly driven by the ever-increasing number of extreme broadband applications and services. First there are many opportunities, since spectrum allocations have been and will be offered for millimeter wavelengths (10 mm to 1 mm) and frequencies (30 to 300 GHz) for wireless mobile communication. Second, important development tools have now been prepared for the millimeter wave spectrum, including channel models, link level and system level simulation (LLS and SLS), antenna and baseband, and radio front-end design. The third source of this growth is that applications are now being planned or developed for these frequencies that go far beyond those already in the market, like automotive radar, wireless broadband fixed access, and satellite communications. Finally there is the unbelievable development and progress of semiconductor technology that will make the implementation of millimeter wave communication feasible for 5G.

In the past, millimeter wave radio frequency technology was the domain of exclusive and low-yield technologies such as GaAs and InP, which had very limited integration capabilities, aiming for professional and military applications. Now SiGe and CMOS technologies graded for consumer products achieve the performance necessary for millimeter wave frequencies; they provide maximum operation frequencies of several hundred GHz and are rapidly advancing even further. Although CMOS technology as of today has both advantages and drawbacks compared to SiGe, CMOS has the lowest cost in volume production and the highest level of integration with digital baseband and even with mixed-signal and radio-frequency front ends. This huge momentum behind CMOS, stemming from the microprocessor mass market and driven by Moore's law, is a reason to have confidence that CMOS technologies will dominate in the millimeter wave frequencies in 5G, implementing a fully integrated millimeter wave communication system consisting of antennas, radio-frequency front end, mixed signal and digital baseband.

© Intel Corp. 2016
B. Badic et al., *Rolling Out 5G*, DOI 10.1007/978-1-4842-1506-7_6

This chapter will give an overview of the use of millimeter frequency bands as part of the next generation cellular systems spectrum. Because millimeter wave technology is gaining increased momentum in the industry and academia, the chapter will provide state-of-the-art insight into a technology considered an important component in enabling high-capacity small cells [30].

The Motivation for Millimeter Wave Usage

In the past and with current technologies, millimeter wave signals have been considered unsuitable for mobile radio access, because of the propagation losses at such high frequencies and their poor propagation through and around obstacles. But considered as a key 5G technology enabler and disruptor, millimeter wave technology will operate in frequencies above 30 GHz (frequencies above 6 GHz are commonly included). Millimeter wave technology inherently provides the bandwidth for extreme broadband communication, but it needs measures to handle its high propagation loss and exposure to blockage from buildings and other objects like raindrops.

Advances in signal processing, driven by Moore's law, currently offer the opportunity to use millimeter wave bands for mobile radio access to improve capacity in constrained geographies. Bands above 6 GHz have already been used for point-to-point (P2P) and line-of-sight (LOS) use cases, such as indoor data streaming or outdoor backhaul access. But the real challenge is being able to implement technologies that can allow millimeter wave signals to operate in non-line-of-sight (NLOS) in mobile radio access scenarios where the devices are moving around. This might be overcome by building multiple-element, dynamic beamforming antenna arrays, which are made possible by the short wavelengths of millimeter wave signals and will be small enough to fit into access points as well as in mobile user equipment (UE).

In addition, short transmission paths and high propagation losses facilitate spectrum re-use in small-cell deployments by limiting the amount of interference between adjacent cells; this in turn improves spectrum efficiency. Where longer paths are required, the extremely short millimeter wavelengths make it possible for very small antennas to concentrate signals into highly focused beams with sufficient gain to overcome propagation losses.

The Spectrum Crunch

With the proliferation of smartphones connected to 3G and 4G networks, wireless data traffic has grown tremendously, by 65 percent between the third quarter (Q3) of 2014 and Q3 2015 [7]. This surge in wireless data traffic was first described as creating a spectrum crunch in 2012 [6]. More recently, ITU-R published the report ITU-R M.2370 "IMT Traffic estimates for the years 2020 to 2030" [18] in July, 2015 to update its views of the marketplace for IMT and to adapt to the traffic forecasts toward the years 2020. This report estimates a global International Mobile Communications (IMT) traffic growth in the range 10–100 times for the years 2020 to 2030, with a growing asymmetry ratio of mobile broadband toward downlink due to video.

As shown in Figure 6-1, total mobile data traffic is projected to increase at a compound annual growth rate (CAGR) of around 45 percent between 2015 and 2021 says Ericsson [7]. Cisco forecasts a CAGR of around 57 percent for mobile data traffic between 2014 and 2019 [9].

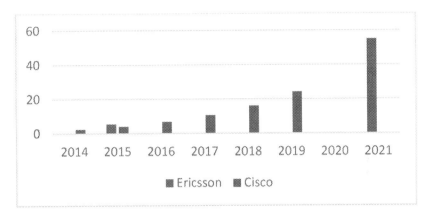

Figure 6-1. *Mobile data (PB per month)*

The Capacity Challenge

There may be many key technology enablers for 5G that will solve the spectrum crunch problem, but one thing is clear about network capacity. It's mainly based upon the available wireless bandwidth; there simply needs to be enough of it. One of the key advantages of millimeter wave technology is the wide spectral bandwidth available. The bandwidth available in the 70 GHz and 80 GHz bands, a total of 10 GHz, is more than the sum total of all other licensed spectrum available for wireless communication. With such wide bandwidth available, millimeter wave wireless links can achieve capacities as high as 10 Gbps in full duplex, which is unlikely to be matched by any lower-frequency RF wireless technologies. The availability of this extraordinary amount of bandwidth also means that the capacity of millimeter wave wireless links can be scaled as demanded by market needs. Typical millimeter wave products commonly available today operate with a spectral efficiency close to 0.5 bits/Hz. However, as the demand arises for higher-capacity links, millimeter wave technology will be able to meet the higher demand by using more efficient modulation schemes.

The millimeter wave bands will be particularly valuable in supporting very–high-capacity networks in areas that need such capacity. Millimeter wave technology will go hand in hand with other 5G technology enablers like advanced antenna systems, adaptive coding and modulation, multi-radio access technology, and advanced small cell networks.

One of the first European research and development projects, the MiWEBA project [22]—a joint undertaking of European and Japanese partners—took the challenge to investigate heterogeneous networks (HetNet), in which millimeter wave ultra-broadband small cells are integrated into cellular networks. The objective was to increase network capacity 1000 times without increasing power consumption and infrastructure deployment cost by 2020. Project system-level simulation results showed in 2015 that the MiWEBA HetNet architecture with appropriate radio resource management algorithms can accomplish in realistic scenarios a gain of more than 1000 times in system rate by installing, for example, 15 millimeter wave small-cell BSes at 60 GHz bands per macro cell area [23]. The project found that location-based cell and beam discovery and selection are critical in particular for implementing resource optimizations and forming a self-organizing network (SON) and to control energy efficiency. So the simulations showed that a thousand-fold system rate increase, from around 120 Mbps for a homogeneous network to around 195 Gbps for the millimeter wave HetNet, could be achieved with a 2× power consumption compared to the legacy homogenous network. Dynamically switching small cells on and off according to their data traffic demand will offer another option to lower power consumption. Additionally, it was found that a dynamic cell structuring scheme that dynamically follows, for example, hotspot zones and assigns idle network resources to them might boost the network capacity even further.

Standardization and Regulation Status

Standardization and regulation of millimeter wave is a complex debate with a wide range of possible options, band combinations, and competing 5G ecosystem stakeholder interests.

The multiplicity of frequency band plan options, including carrier aggregation (CA), for the 5G predecessors is already very complex. The complexity is based on performance requirements and additional regionally specific performance characteristics, like out-of-band (OOB) emissions. The extension of mobile cellular communications systems to higher centimeter frequency bands like 2400 MHz and 3400-3800 MHz has already made necessary coexistence spectrum management with satellite and radar systems, which brings along additional cost and complexity and occasionally performance degradation. Extending this further into the upper end of the centimeter band and the lower millimeter band for 5G systems leads to related coexistence challenges with mobile satellite, back haul and front-haul service providers, and auto radar all asking for solutions to keep the cost and performance impact economically feasible.

IEEE 802.11ad and 802.11ay

The objective of the IEEE project 802.11ad [15] was to amend the 802.11 physical layers (PHY) and the 802.11 Medium Access Control Layer (MAC) for operation in the 57–66 GHz frequency band providing up to 7 Gbps data throughput. The standard was approved in October, 2012. The first products became available, for example, from Intel in 2015 and further ones are announced for 2016.

IEEE project 802.11ay was started in March, 2015 to develop another amendment to IEEE 802.11 PHY and MAC that allows at least one mode of operation capable of supporting a maximum data throughput of at least 20 Gbps and operation for license-exempt bands above 45 GHz while ensuring backward-compatibility and coexistence with IEEE 802.11ad operating in the same band. Use cases [14] are

- Ultra-short range communications (up to 0.1 m, ~10 Gbps)

- 8K UHD video streaming (up to 5 m, up to 28 Gbps)

- AR/VR devices (up to 5 m, ~20 Gbps)

- Data center inter-rack links (up to 10 m, ~20 Gbps)

- UHD video broadcast (up to 100 m, up to 20 Gbps), mobile data offloading (up to 100 m, up to 20 Gbps)

- Wireless front-haul (up to 200 m, up to 20 Gbps)wireless back haul (up to 150 m single hop, ~ 2 Gbps)

- Office docking (up to 3 m, up to 20 Gbps)

A first version of the amendment draft is planned to be available in May 2017.

3GPP

The 3GPP is collaboration between groups of telecommunications associations. Its scope is the development of standards including 2G (GPRS, EDGE), 3G (UMTS), 4G (LTE, LTE-A) and now 5G. 3GPP standardization incorporates radio access network (RAN), core network and terminals (CT), and service architecture (SA). The work on 5G started in September 2015 with a workshop [3] where more than 70 presentations from ecosystem stakeholders disclosed a huge spectrum of requirements for use cases like enhanced mobile broadband (eMBB), massive machine type communications (mMTC), and ultra-reliable and low-latency communication (uMTC). The specifications for the next generation of mobile broadband access will come in two phases, where the first phase will be completed in the second half of 2018 (3GPP Release 15), and the second phase will finish by end of 2019 (3GPP Release 16) (3GPP, 2015).

A majority of partners in 3GPP came to the agreement that there will be a new radio access technology (RAT) that will not be backward compatible. Therefore, new study items are kicked off to specify scenarios and requirements for this new RAT and to evaluate technology solutions including millimeter wave.

ETSI ISG mWT

In the European standards body ETSI an industry specification group on millimeter wave transmission (ISG mWT) started in January, 2015 to investigate the use of millimeter wave technology for backhaul and front-haul connections as an important building block in an upcoming 5G system. The focus is on millimeter wave bands at 57–66 GHz (V-band), 71–76 GHz, and 81–86 GHz (E-band) and on delivering maximum contiguous bandwidth for use cases like the following:

- Macro-cell mobile backhaul applications (mobile network upgrade, expansion)

- Small-cell mobile backhaul application (rooftop-to-street/street-to-street connectivity, multi-hop)

- Front-haul for small cells applications (rooftop-to-street/street-to-street connectivity, multi-hop)

- Front-haul for macro cells applications (mobile network upgrade, expansion),

- Fixed broadband radio access (wireless to the home, wireless to the cabinet)

and others [11]. An analysis [10] of antenna requirements compared to the capabilities of current antenna solutions (parabolic, lens, waveguide, PCB) targeting these use cases shows there are still challenges regarding performance (gain) and features (such as obtrusiveness).

FCC and CEPT

The US Federal Communications Commission (FCC) is piloting the discussion of band availability above 24 GHz in particular millimeter wave bands (Figure 6-2). This includes collecting input from many 5G ecosystem stakeholders. The FCC is examining higher-frequency bands for the next generation of wireless services, including millimeter wave in particular, to develop a regulatory framework to support 5G mobile services [12]. The focus is currently on bands that have an existing mobile allocation: these are 27.5–28.35 GHz (the 28 GHz band), 38.6–40 GHz (the 39 GHz band), 37–38.6 GHz (the 37 GHz band), and the 64–71 GHz band.

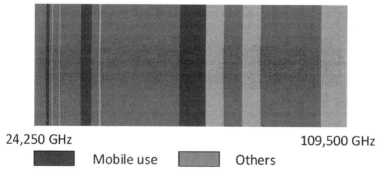

24,250 GHz   109,500 GHz

▓▓▓▓ Mobile use   ▒▒▒▒ Others

Figure 6-2. *FCC bands above 24 GHz for possible mobile use*

Existing incumbent uses must be considered when selecting these millimeter wave bands for mobile use. The first feedback from ecosystem stakeholders revealed the need for a substantial amount of contiguous bandwidth to enable 5G services; this contiguous bandwidth ranges from 500 MHz to 2 GHz. The FCC proposes a geographic area licensing scheme that is flexible to provide access and protection for fixed, mobile, and FSS uses in the 28 GHz and 39 GHz band. It suggests a licensing model that attempts to maximize the use of spectrum by creating rights for both local area networks and wide area networks in the 37 GHz band.

The European Conference of Postal and Telecommunications Administrations (CEPT) and other European and Asian regulatory agencies have discussions under way in quest of spectrum favorites above 6 GHz, but the process is slow and affected by a wide range of national regulator opinions and widespread industry special interests. CEPT manages all European telecommunication issues by facilitating European regulators and deploying ITU policies in accordance with European goals. Wireless matters are done by the Electronic Communications Committee (ECC), which does the frequency management and spectrum engineering. The ECC's Conference Preparatory Group (CPG) is in charge of developing briefs, studies, and European Common Proposals (ECPs) for the world radio communication conference (WRC) and prepared several proposals for IMT above 6 GHz in 2015, all of them above 28 GHz.

ITU-R WP5A and WP5D

The world radio conferences (WRC) of ITU-R, which decides the changes in the spectrum use, take place about every 3 to 4 years. ITU-R member states make the decisions. The WRC 2015 took place in November, 2015 in Geneva, gathering around 3800 participants representing 162 member states and 130 other entities including industry. Agenda items (AI) comprise the conclusions; their outcome impacts spectrum above 6 GHz (Figure 6-3). So AI 1.1 agreed upon additional spectrum for international mobile telecommunications (IMT) at 470– 694/698, 1427–1518, 3300–3400, 3400–3600, 3600–3700, and 4800–4990 MHz. AI 1.2 decided on 694–790 MHz for mobile allocation and identification for IMT confirmed in R1, with conditions that are similar to those of 800 MHz for IMT in Region 1. AI 1.3 asked administrations to consider parts of the frequency range 694–894 MHz for public safety (PS). AI 10 agreed on spectrum above 6 GHz for some bands between 24–84 GHz to be studied.

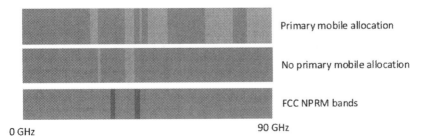

Figure 6-3. *Bands above 6 GHz to be studied toward WRC-19*

Spectrum below 6 GHz was also newly identified for regions as well as key markets. Previously identified bands like 3.4–3.6 GHz and 700 MHz bands were upgraded to global or near-global status, but there is also general discontent about the small amount of new spectrum identified and its disparity among regions. Some ecosystem stakeholders challenge the effectiveness and ROI of using the ITU for future IMT spectrum. The need to focus on key markets was stressed as current plans in Korea, Japan, China, and the US are very demanding. Key bands identified below 6 GHz are already on the 3GPP roadmap; however, ITU-R's WRC-15 did not provide an obvious harmonized band for deployment of 5G for global coverage.

And there is spectrum above 6 GHz, where bands have been agreed for study toward WRC-19 through TG5/1. For example, the status of the 28 GHz band was challenged regarding the exclusion of the band from the ITU list of bands to be studied by comments from US and Korea who want to perform 5G trials at 28 GHz in a 2017–2018 timeframe. The discussion of identifying future IMT spectrum is important, in particular looking at its impact on future 5G spectrum and the existing strong opposition in ITU for several target bands both below and above 6 GHz.

For example, looking at the current work plan of WP5D in light of the outcome of WRC-15 and upcoming studies including spectrum estimation, development of sharing parameters, and modeling of IMT-2020 for sharing studies, it seems there is a need for some adjustments to deadlines. So some ecosystem stakeholders are considering alternative mechanisms such as working in regional groups and direct contact with regulators, especially in larger markets, as well as preparatory work in industry forums harmonizing outside the ITU and upfront as much as possible.

There was an agreement in principle on an agenda item for WRC-19 on spectrum for 5G (IMT-2020). But the studies and decisions by WRC-19 are limited to bands above 24 GHz as follows: 24.25–27.5 GHz, 37–40.5 GHz, 42.5–43.5 GHz, 45.5–47 GHz, 47.2–50.2 GHz, 50.4–52.6 GHz, 66–76 GHz, and 81–86 GHz are bands already allocated to mobile service in the table of allocations, and the bands 31.8– 33.4 GHz, 40.5–42.5 GHz and 47–47.2 GHz would require a new allocation to mobile service in the table of allocations. It has to be taken into account that not all of these bands and/or not the full bands will be identified for IMT by WRC-19. A new ITU group TG5/1 has been established to study coexistence of 5G with existing uses of these bands.

Bands above 6 GHz listed for study were mostly chosen based on inclusion in regional proposals to WRC-15 as a simple common denominator. Band 27.5–29.5 GHz was extensively debated with strong support from US, Japan, Korea, Sweden, Finland, and some other countries, but was finally not included in the list of bands to be studied toward WRC-19 because of opposition from others. This band faced the strongest opposition from the satellite industry speaking for various countries. Nonetheless, the ecosystem stakeholders will continue working on the 27.5–29.5 GHz and 6–24 GHz band ranges, because there are already research results on channel model and industry development and prototyping done, for example, at 28 GHz more than in any other high band. And mobile services only need to coexist with fixed terrestrial services and FSS Uplink (only aggregate interference to satellites is to be addressed), while other bands are generally encumbered with other types of space services or are adjacent to passive bands.

Nevertheless, ITU-R working party 5D (WP5D) will conduct studies (Figure 6-4) on the topics of spectrum needs and technical and operational characteristics, including protection criteria, planning to deploy scenarios by end of March 2017. The characteristics need to be applicable over the frequency range of 24–86 GHz. The sharing and compatibility studies will take place within TG5/1 and must be completed in spring or autumn 2018. The technical and operational characteristics include transmit power for both access point (AP) and user equipment (UE), directivity of transmission (for a traditional AP, this is the antenna pattern, whereas for Multiple Input, Multiple Output (MIMO), it will become more complex), spectrum emission masks, and the receiver C/I performance for protection criteria. Propagation models will be developed in ITU-R Study Group 3 in parallel with propagation models from 3GPP.

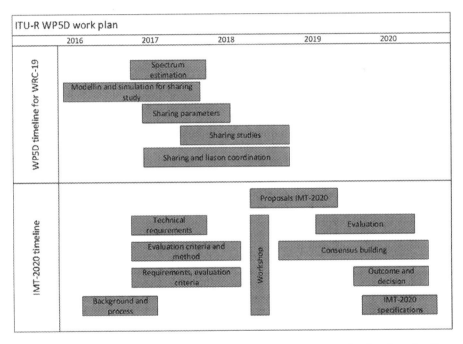

Figure 6-4. *ITU-R WP5D work plan combined view on spectrum and technology timelines*

Channel Models

There is rising attention in using millimeter wave bands for 5G mobile wireless networks. Channel models are of utmost importance for measurement campaigns, channel model characterization, system-level simulations, and network access capacity estimations in particular for 5G, which is planned to integrate new frequency bands above 6 GHz. A radio channel model includes the antenna effects (almost all models are of this type), whereas a propagation channel model removes antenna effects and is therefore valid for any antenna type. The latter has the disadvantage of requiring different models for the uplink and downlink channel.

The absolute challenge for a channel model is to have just one channel model with adjustable parameters for all scenarios and propagation effects for the full frequency range from above 6 GHz up to 100 GHz. A practicable approach is to develop a sound collection of 3D channel models for the most likely deployment scenarios [28]. Identified typical deployment scenarios are

- 3D-urban micro (UMi), such as the open area shown in Figure 6-5 and street canyon shown in Figure 6-6), comprising both outdoor-to-outdoor (O2O) and outdoor to indoor (O2I)

- Indoor (InH, such as open and closed offices and the shopping malls shown in Figure 6-7)

- 3D-urban macro (UMa), comprising O2O and O2I, backhaul for small cells, device-to-device (D2D), and vehicle-to-anything (V2X)

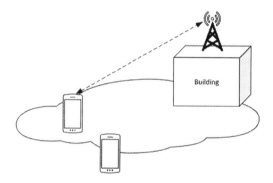

Figure 6-5. *3D-UMi O2O open-area scenario*

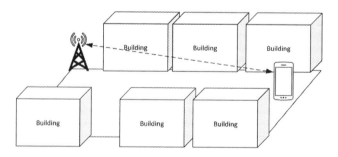

Figure 6-6. *3D-UMi O2O open-area street canyon scenario*

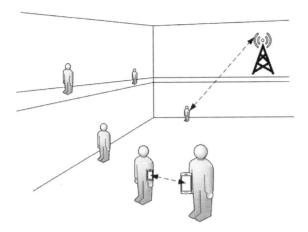

Figure 6-7. InH shopping mall scenario

To build a channel model requires data either from measurements in the field or derived from ray tracing. Hence, there have been numerous measurement campaigns over several years, and more are being currently set up, to characterize the millimeter wave communication channel for various specific outdoor and indoor environments. Using the data sets gathered will then make possible several approaches to addressing challenges like the following:

- The line-of-sight (LOS) and non-line-of-sight NLOS) path loss (PL) model

- Delay and angular spreads

- Shadowing

- Spatial consistency and environment dynamics

- The impact of very large antenna arrays (spherical wave modeling)

- The dual mobility Doppler model for D2D

- The frequency dependency of propagation channel model parameters, due to inadequate available measurement campaign data

- The ratio between diffuse and specular reflections

- Polarization

Channel model parameterization challenges are the estimation of large scale parameters (LSP) like delay spread (DS), angular spreads (AS), Ricean K factor (K) and shadow fading (SF) as well estimation of small scale parameters (SSP). Simulation and implementation challenges are complexity, performance and availability.

Ecosystem stakeholders and projects that have met those challenges and have developed channel models are METIS2020 [21], MiWEBA [13], ITU-R M, COST2100 [8], IEEE 802.11ad [20], NYU Wireless [25], and Fraunhofer HHI QuaDRIGa [19]. The 3GPP Spatial Channel Model (SCM)[1], WINNER [26] and ITU-R IMT-Advanced propagation model guidelines [17] were built on extensive channel-propagation measurement campaigns and apply to frequencies of up to 6 GHz. The IEEE 802.11ad channel model emphasizes the 60 GHz band and an indoor scenario; it is created deterministically, and the parameterization is site-specific. COST 2100 is working on the COST channel model, which exploits measurement campaigns and extracts parameters out of it. QuaDRIGa is modeling MIMO radio channels via ray-tracing for specific network configurations, such as indoor, indoor/outdoor, or outdoor environments implementing a 3D geometry-based stochastic channel model. Currently there are additional ongoing propagation and channel studies at the 5G mmWave Channel Model Alliance (United States, NIST-initiated), mmMagic (Europe), IMT-2020 5G promotion association (China), the ETSI industry specification group on millimeter wave transmission (ISG mWT), and 3GPP.

Many of those channel models are adapted to the 3GPP 3D channel model structure, achieving a good fit with available 3GPP system-level simulation environments. Others model the outdoor wave communication channel, using an approach that is either analytical, statistical, or ray-tracing–based statistical. Figure 6-8 shows an overview of the channel modeling options based on the trade-off between accuracy and simplicity.

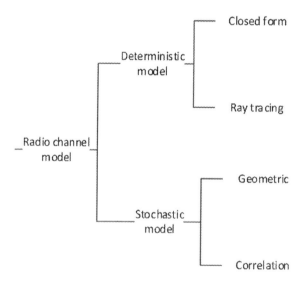

Figure 6-8. *Channel modeling options*

These options for channel modeling can be narrowed down to an extension of the 3GPP 3D model, a map-based model, or something like the hybrid quasi-deterministic model for example from MiWEBA. There is a preference among ecosystem stakeholders for the extension of the 3GPP 3D model by adding features like the following:

- The impact of foliage.

- Atmosphere and rain attenuations as a function of frequency.

- The blockage caused by static and moving objects such as a human body or vehicle. Blockage attenuation generally increases with frequency.

- Spatial consistency, which involves the evolutionary features and the correlation of channels between adjacent UEs or links on the large and small scales, supporting massive MIMO, mobility ,and beam tracking

- Support for large bandwidth and 3D beamforming with antenna arrays consisting of a large number of antennas.

The 3GPP channel model has evolved from the spatial channel model for Multiple Input Multiple Output (MIMO) [4] over several stages to the most recent 3D channel model for LTE [5], all of them for frequencies up to 2.5 GHz. This 3GPP model will be extended to included frequency bands above 6 GHz. 3GPP is conducting a study on a channel model for the frequency spectrum above 6 GHz, approved as RP-151606 "New SID Proposal: Study on channel model for frequency spectrum above 6 GHz" (Samsung, Nokia Networks, 2015), in RAN#69 in September, 2015. From RAN#69 to RAN#70 3GPP TSG RAN identified the status and expectation of existing information about high frequencies, including spectrum allocation, scenarios of interest, measurements, and so on. Beginning in the first quarter 2016, RAN1 will develop a channel model for frequencies up to 100 GHz, taking into account the outcome of RAN-level discussion and discussion in the 3GPP 5G requirement study item (SI). This work will define the additional details of the scenarios of interest required for RAN1 work and will consider the work done outside 3GPP as well as earlier 3GPP work, such as the 3GPP 3D-channel model, as a starting point for the modeling of wireless channels of the high-frequency spectrum for the identified scenarios. Additionally, it will consider the possible implications of the new channel model on the existing 3D channel model for spectrum below 6 GHz.

Research similar to [13] is exploring the remaining open issues, such as dealing with human body shadowing or reflections caused by moving vehicles or attenuation by dense vegetation in cities. For example, Figure 6-9 is a simplified view of how the channel impulse response amplitude of the line of sight path is strongly attenuated by blockage, whereas the amplitude of reflected paths is not. Further exploration is also needed, and under way, to determine in detail when and how millimeter wave systems are noise or interference limited, and the impact of polarization and greater temporal and spatial channel model resolution.

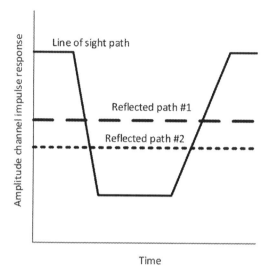

Figure 6-9. *Human body blockage and shadowing*

Enabling Technologies

There are technology challenges in all the building blocks (Figure 6-10) to implement millimeter wave transceivers. First there is the implementation of high-gain adaptive antennas with a small form factor and real-time beam-switching to overcome the propagation loss at millimeter wave bands; these antennas are also needed to address blockage, even in the case of mobility, to ensure continuous connectivity. Further essentials include radio-frequency front ends with up to 2 GHz operational bandwidth, phase shifting capabilities, and power amplifiers that support MIMO with high linearity and viable power efficiency. Finally, a high-performance digital baseband capable of processing several giga-samples per second with power consumption useful for mobile devices is needed to run the 5G protocols.

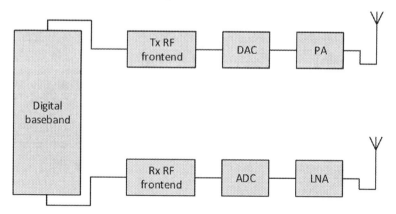

Figure 6-10. *Millimeter wave transceiver building blocks*

Ecosystem stakeholders are working toward new air interfaces as well as new antenna designs based on emerging massive MIMO technology that will become available in 2020. So, for example, LTE-A Pro as well as IEEE 802.11ax will provide more than one Gbps in addition to a new radio access technology based on millimeter wave technology and will be integrated with legacy radios into a transceiver in 2020 (Figure 6-11).

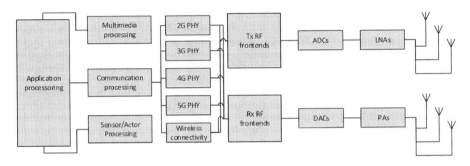

Figure 6-11. *Wireless transceiver in 2020*

Moving in this direction, Intel rolled out an IEEE 802.11ad product for wireless docking stations [16]. The Intel Tri-Band Wireless-AC 17265 client brings 60 GHz 802.11ad wireless docking connectivity for mobile client devices. Combined with the dedicated Intel Wireless Gigabit Antenna-M 10041R antenna module and the Intel Wireless Gigabit Sink-M 13100 wireless dock, it supports a wire-equivalent user experience for wireless docking, access to peripherals, and D2D communications.

Antennas

In designing millimeter-wave communication systems, high-gain antennas are a must-have building block to compensate for the high path loss (inversely proportional to the squared wavelength) and the oxygen absorption coefficient (around 15 dB/km at 60 GHz), both of have stronger effect on data transmission over greater distances. All of these path losses might be offset by higher antenna gain and transmit power. Antennas for millimeter wave frequencies can be built smaller than those for lower bands, an advantage that is very significant in wireless systems, where small antennas are indispensable. But the quest for high antenna gain requires a large antenna aperture that scales proportionally to the wavelength square and creates a boundary condition. Reducing the physical size of the millimeter wave antennas raises the issues of heat dissipation and losses in thin feeding lines.

The high antenna gain required to improve the link budget creates very narrow beams, which means the antennas of the transmitter and receiver have to be perfectly adjusted; this is done by beam steering and beam tracking in milliseconds in case of AP and/or UE mobility. Among many options to build antenna arrays there are two major ones to build a millimeter wave phased antenna array (PAA), which will be discussed further shortly. One is example of the PAA is the modular antenna array

(MAA), and another is the lens array antenna (LAA); both are verified to be practicable as implementation options for highly-directional steerable millimeter wave antennas for the 5G roll out.

PAAs in millimeter wave bands consist of multiple antenna elements each of which has its own phase shifter. Phase shifters allow us to control the antenna pattern by adjusting phases of the signal on each antenna element. The gain of the PAA depends on the number of antenna elements, but the antenna pattern is also defined by the antenna element configuration. A block diagram for the transceiver using the PAA is shown in Figure 6-12. The transmitter (TX) includes digital baseband (BB), digital-to-analog converter (DAC), and a radio-frequency front-end (RFE), which consists of phase shifters and power amplifiers (PA) for each antenna and the antenna array itself.

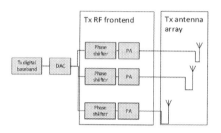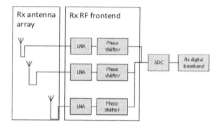

Figure 6-12. *PAA overview*

The benefit of PAAs is that the antenna array gain is proportional to the number of antenna elements. Their properties work well for interference rejection, they have good receive sensitivity, and they support fast multi-beam scanning. But the model requires a large number of antenna elements, which must be connected with phase shifters, amplifiers, and antenna elements. These connections could lead to losses and impedance mismatch, which could distort phase, and finally to a deterioration of the antenna performance.

LAA, the other implementation option for millimeter wave antennas, contains a discrete lens and a feeding source placed in the focal plane—usually a directional antenna (Figure 6-13).

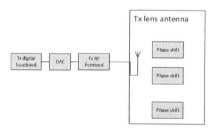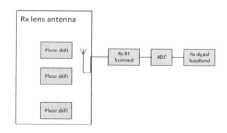

Figure 6-13. *LAA overview*

PAA and LAA are currently being improved further in particular for backhaul and front-haul millimeter wave applications, since the antenna requirements for access regarding transmit power, antenna gain, beam steering capability, physical size and cost are by far more challenging. To this end Intel has developed a modular antenna array (MAA) [29] such as shown in Figure 6-14, which consists of multiple independent antenna subarrays, where each subarray has its own phase-shifting circuitry and RFE.

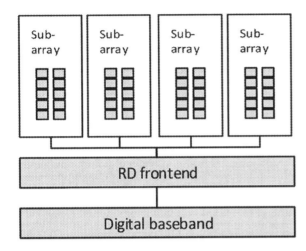

Figure 6-14. *MAA overview*

This basic antenna array module (Figure 6-15) has dimensions of around 9 mm × 25 mm and could be populated with 2 × 10 antenna elements, for example [31]. In the middle of the array (shown in yellow) 2 × 8 elements are used to generate a radiation pattern required for directive transmission (beamforming). One element (blue) performs an omnidirectional transmission, and three other elements (white) are there for further subarray extensions.

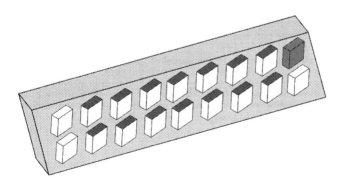

Figure 6-15. *Intel basic antenna array module*

Radio-Frequency Front Ends

The current technology for millimeter wave radio-frequency front ends is focused so far mainly on two architecture options, the heterodyne architecture and the direct conversion architecture. Mixed-signal, frequency generation, modulation, and conversion, as well as power amplifiers are building blocks common to both architectures. The receiver chain comprises low-noise amplifiers (LNAs), an analog-digital-converter (ADC), filters, mixers, and frequency generators. The transmit chain consists of filters, mixers, digital-analog-converter (DAC), and power amplifier (PA). The filters in the transceiver are there to reject unwanted spectral content. The mixers are used to modulate a frequency carrier signal with the local oscillator (LO) signal. Implementing a millimeter wave radio front end as heterodyne architecture has the advantage that both the frequency generation and the modulation block work at an intermediate frequency (IF) that will be much lower than the millimeter wave carrier frequency and therefore has lower power consumption, less phase noise requirements, and relaxed calibration efforts. However, the heterodyne transmitter needs a band-pass filter for image rejection after the up-conversion; this is difficult to implement because of its filter bandwidth and steepness requirements. The other option, the direction conversion architecture, does not need the image reducing band-pass filter but faces challenges in building block calibration and in compensating for parasitic feedback, for example from the PA, frequency generator, and mixer.

Phase shifters, as discussed in the section "Antennas," are an essential component in a phased array for adjusting the phase of each antenna path and steering the beam. The requirements of phase shifters include large phase-control range, high phase-shift resolution, low insertion loss, low variations in loss over all phase states, and the like. It is challenging to design radio frequency phase shifters at millimeter wave frequencies in a CMOS technology [27]. Some phase shifters, such as the switched-line and switched-filter types, suffer from the limited performance of MOSFET switches. Other phase shifters, such as reflection-type and traveling-wave, often have high insertion losses and large variations in losses.

Among the most challenging blocks are the amplifiers needed to achieve highest integration levels in CMOS, which takes into account both the low noise amplifier (LNA) at the radio receiver and high power and high efficiency power amplifier (PA) at the radio transmitter. The design challenges for LNA and PA are related to the CMOS drawbacks, like low breakdown voltages of CMOS transistors, the low supply voltages, the high gain and efficiency needs over a wide band, the mitigation of process variations, the control of the noise figures, and (last but not least) the thermal conditions.

Finally, the implementation of multi-user and massive MIMO techniques in millimeter wave radio transceivers with large antenna arrays at viable power consumption drastically increases the number of transceiver chains, from the currently 2 to 4 for up to 4×4 MIMO, and therefore requires innovative trade-offs regarding radio front-end combining architectures, where several radio frequency front ends support more than one antenna and the mixed signal is designed for low power, feeding a power-efficient digital baseband.

Baseband and Protocols

The economics of the 5G system will be substantiated among others in scheduling, modulation, coding, and multiplexing options, which have to support spectral efficiency, low delay, and high variability in data throughput over a huge variety of frequency bands including millimeter wave bands. There is no one-size-fits-all protocol, and the challenge is to provide a solution with an efficient trade-off between spectral and power efficiency so that the protocol itself is then adapted for meter, centimeter, and millimeter wave band. For example, looking retrospectively at the 5G predecessors' modulation schemes we can already see similar smart trade-offs.

2G GMSK modulation is not on the whole spectrally efficient but works well in the power domain and is efficient with CMOS power amplifiers. Spectral efficiency is achieved through a well-balanced mixture of bandwidth-efficient voice codecs and digital coding gain based on block and convolutional coding. Then 3G changes the method to higher-order QPSK and 16 QAM modulation, which improves spectral efficiency but works less well in the power domain. Coding gain is used as in 2G but comes at the expense of more processing clock cycles to equalize the wider channel bandwidth. 4G adds OFDM for coping with a nonconstant channel frequency response, where modulation and demodulation are made computationally efficient via FFT. OFDM also allows for more complex space frequency time coding, with several frequency subcarriers and antenna elements. So OFDM is in many ways elegant; the challenges to extending it to millimeter wave are the cyclic prefix (CP) absorbing bandwidth and power, the high requirements regarding phase noise and OOB emissions, and at-large resource block allocation. Regarding coding there are various options including parity checks, block and convolutional codes, turbo, low-density parity check codes (LDPC), and polar codes to deliver sensitivity and selectivity gain.

References

1. 3GPP. (2012-09). Technical Specification Group Radio Access Network; Spatial channel model for Multiple Input Multiple Output (MIMO) simulations. 3GPP TR 25.996 V11.0.0.
2. 3GPP. (2015). 3GPP timeline 5G. Retrieved from 3GPP: http://www.3gpp.org/ftp/tsg_sa/tsg_sa/TSGS_67/Docs/SP-150149.zip
3. 3GPP. (2015, October 19). RAN 5G Workshop. Retrieved from 3GPP: http://www.3gpp.org/news-events/3gpp-news/1734-ran_5g
4. 3GPP TR 25.996. (2015). Spatial channel model for Multiple Input Multiple Output (MIMO) simulations. 3GPP.
5. 3GPP TR 36.873. (2015). Study on 3D channel model for LTE. 3GPP.
6. CEA Spectrum report—the White House. (2012). The economic benefits of new spectrum for wireless broadband. Washington D.C.: Executive office of the president council of economic advisers.
7. Cisco. (2015). Cisco Visual Networking Index: Forecast and Methodology, 2014. Cisco.
8. COST. (2014). COST. Retrieved from COST: http://www.cost2100.org/
9. Ericsson. (2015). Ericsson Mobility Report. Stockholm: Ericsson.
10. ETSI. (2015). Analysis of antennas for millimeter wave transmission. ETSI ISG mWT.
11. ETSI ISG mWT. (2015). Applications and use cases of millimeter wave transmission. ETSI.

12. FCC. (2015). Notice of proposed rule making. FCC-15-138A1.
13. Fraunhofer HHI. (2014). Channel modeling and characterization. MiWEBA.
14. IEEE 11-15/0625r3. (2015). IEEE 802.11 TGay use cases. IEEE.
15. IEEE. (2012). 802.11ad-Amendment 3: Enhancements for Very High Throughput in the 60 GHz Band. IEEE Standard for Information technology.
16. Intel. (2015). Intel wireless docking. Retrieved from Intel: http://www.intel.com/content/www/us/en/wireless-products/wireless-docking.html
17. ITU-R. (2009). Guidelines for evaluation of radio interface technologies for IMT-Advanced, International telecommunication union (ITU), Geneva, Switzerland, Technical Report. ITU-R M.2135-1.
18. ITU-R. (2015). IMT traffic estimates for the years 2020 to 2030. ITU-R M.2370-0.
19. Jaeckel, S., Raschkowski, L., Börner, K., & Thiele, L. (2014). "QuaDRiGa: A 3-D Multicell Channel Model with Time Evolution for Enabling Virtual Field Trials". IEEE Trans. Antennas Propag.
20. Maltsev, A., Erceg, V., Perahia, E., Hansen, C., Maslennikov, R., Lomayev, A., Harada, H. (2010). Channel Models for 60 GHz WLAN Systems. IEEE 802.11ad 09/0334r8.
21. METIS2020. (2015). METIS Channel Model. METIS2020.
22. MiWEBA. (2013). Retrieved from http://www.miweba.eu/#Project
23. MiWEBA. (2015). D4.5 Overall system performance evaluation results. MiWEBA.
24. Samsung, Nokia Networks. (2015, Sep). Contributions. Retrieved from 3GPP: https://portal.3gpp.org/ngppapp/TdocList.aspx?meetingId=31198
25. T. S. Rappaport, e. a. (2015). Wideband Millimeter-Wave Propagation Measurements and Channel Models for Future Wireless Communication System Design. IEEE Transactions on Communications, 3029-3056.
26. WINNER. (2010). WINNER II Channel Models 2007; D5.3: WINNER+ Final Channel Models 2010. IST-4-027756 D1.1.2 V1.2.
27. Y. Yu, P. G. (2011). Integrated 60GHz RF Beamforming in CMOS. Heidelberg London New York: Springer.
28. Maltsev A., Pudeyev A., Karls I., Bolotin I., Morozov G., Weiler R.J., Peter M., Keusgen W., "Quasi-deterministic Approach to mmWave Channel Modeling in a Non-stationary Environment", IEEE GLOBECOM 2014, Austin, Texas, USA, pp966-971.
29. Maltsev A., Sadri A., Pudeyev A., Bolotin I., Davydov A., Morozov G., Weiler R., "Partially Adaptive Arrays application for MU-MIMO mode in a MmWave Small Cells", IEEE PIMRC2015, pp315-319.
30. Maltsev A., Sadri A., Pudeyev A., Bolotin I., Davydov A., Morozov G., "Performance evaluation of the MmWave Small Cells communication system in MU-MIMO mode", EuCNC'2015.
31. Maltsev A., Sadri A., Pudeyev A., Bolotin I., "Highly-directional steerable antennas", IEEE Vehicular Technology Magazine, March 2016.

Conclusion

This book has introduced the requirements for the next generation of mobile cellular systems and the challenges to rolling out such systems. We started with an overview of the evolution of cellular systems, detailing how 2G, 3G, and 4G wireless communication were designed for person-to-person communication, improving speed and efficiency with every new generation. Following that introduction, we then discussed why 5G will be different—in terms of implementation challenges and novel enablers of 5G, like network densification, millimeter wave technology, machine-type communications, device-to-device communications, and virtualization techniques. This new framework will finally lead to billions of connected devices that are projected to be deployed in the mid- and long-term while maintaining and even increasing speed and resource efficiency.

Many of the future requirements can already be met by LTE-Advanced Pro, as emphasized in the first part of this book. Moore's Law is enabling an ever-increased integration density of cellular modems, already today leading to peak data rates in the hundreds of Mbps, and it is allowing concentration of network signal processing complexity centrally in a Cloud RAN. Interference handling will see an increase in sophistication and complexity, with network-based interference management and terminal-based interference mitigation algorithms. LTE-Advanced Pro capacity and coverage will increase through the use of LTE in unlicensed spectrum, increased flexibility of the LTE frame structure, a greater number of carriers, and more antennas at the base station. At the same time, a growing demand in IoT and wearable systems is bringing tremendous advances in user experience, applications, and overall system efficiency.

A straightforward evolution of the existing technology will thus be able to meet our demands for a few more years, but the time will soon come that requires a true revolution: future applications will continue to require more spectrum, more data, and more intelligence in communication systems. The communication networks will have to be fundamentally altered to provide the immense computing and communications power required to leverage that surge in connected devices. 5G networks will be smarter and more efficient to support each type of radio spectrum and each type of device, from the simple sensor to the sophisticated self-driving car. From embedded devices in all kinds of equipment to autonomous vehicles and drones, smart enterprises and cities, 5G networks will connect things to each other, to persons, and the cloud. Billions of increasingly smart and connected devices, data-rich personalized services, and cloud applications are setting the requirements for a smarter, more powerful, and more efficient 5G network. The transition to this 5G network is finally bringing computing and

© Intel Corp. 2016
B. Badic et al., *Rolling Out 5G*, DOI 10.1007/978-1-4842-1506-7

communications together. Industry partnerships with computing and communication ecosystem leaders are laying the foundation for future 5G networks now to make amazing user experiences possible in the future. It starts with these ecosystem leaders joining forces on pre-standard 5G radio technologies and network solutions to enable early implementation of both 5G mobile devices and wireless network infrastructure, as well as interoperability of 5G radio technologies to meet the device connectivity requirements for wireless networks mid- and long-term. Computing and communication industry leaders are developing and verifying 5G mobile device and network solutions for centimeter and millimeter wave bands including spectrum sharing in unlicensed spectrum bands. The industry is also working on advances in radio access network technologies, including anchor-booster cell and massive MIMO to further improve 5G wireless network capacity.

New, highly integrated modems, antennas, and highly sophisticated systems-on-chips are required to provide robust connectivity for IoT, mobile devices, and PCs. Chipset suppliers already offer 5G mobile trial platforms to develop early high-performance prototype solutions that put 5G development on a fast-track. Chipset suppliers, infrastructure providers, and mobile network operators are collaborating on these 5G mobile trial platforms to drive network transformation, the cloud, and IoT.

Furthermore, the network setup and related business models are about to change dramatically. An upside-down reshuffling of the entire industry is on our doorstep. As illustrated in the accompanying figure, we will abandon the large scale deployment of infrastructure hardware components.

Today

Future

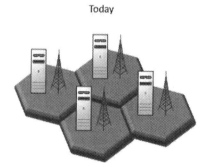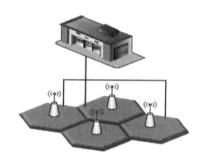

The network infrastructure of the future

In-the-field base stations will disappear, as corresponding processing functionalities are moved to remote data centers and only remote antenna heads remain in the field, complemented by Mobile Edge Computing (MEC) capabilities—fed by optical-fiber links or high-rate wireless connections to the data centers. Finally, cloud computing converges to fog computing where the right mixture of centralized and distributed processing elements is used.

On the technical side, this approach allows for highly efficient joint processing of all cells performing near-perfect interference mitigation. Thanks to Network-Function-Virtualization (NFV) and Software-Defined Networking (SDN), computational resources will be allocated just where they are needed, preferably to be adopted on a short-term basis. Any major maintenance tasks are performed centrally at the data center, and experts no longer need to be sent out into the field. Software to be executed in the data centers is expected to largely build on open source solutions, possibly combined with proprietary security modules, and thus lead to a massive cost reduction.

From a business model perspective, this vision will be an entire game changer. Network operators will typically no longer own any spectrum or infrastructure—instead, all spectrum and computational resources will be rented on a per-need basis, possibly in a highly dynamic fashion taking local capacity needs and user behavior into account. New stakeholders that are deploying and leasing hardware and spectrum resources to operators will arise.

A typical example is a short-term, large-scale event, such as a football match. Most of the time, a stadium is empty and no major wireless traffic is occuring. During this time, a minimum of spectrum and computational resources are assigned to the concerned geographic area. During a match, this situation changes dramatically—tens of thousands of people will enjoy the match, access social media, share real time video, and so on. During this limited time, massive spectrum and computational resources will be allocated to this specific geographic area in order to meet the user demands.

To sum up, while ensuring that 4G LTE-Advanced Pro satisfies current and near-future user demands, the work toward 5G will continue: ultra-fast data transfer speeds, low communication latency, higher network capacity, and increased energy efficiency to support 5G applications, wearables, and IoT systems.

Index

A

Active Antenna Systems (AAS), 48
Almost Blank Subframes (ABS), 20
Analog-digital-converter (ADC), 128
Angular spreads (AS), 121

B

Block error rates (BLER), 30

C

Component carriers (CCs), 18
Compound annual growth
    rate (CAGR), 113
Cross-carrier scheduling (CCS), 24

D

Delay spread (DS), 121
Device-to-device
    communication (D2D), 8, 61
Digital-to-analog converter (DAC), 126
Domain manager (DM), 96

E

Element manager (EM), 96
Enhanced Machine-to-machine
    communication (eMTC), 8
Enhanced NodeB (eNB), 14
European Conference of Postal and
    Telecommunications
    Administrations (CEPT), 117
Extreme mobile broadband (xMBB), 8, 53

F

Frequency division
    duplex (FDD), 80, 89
Frequency Domain Multiple Access
    Frequency Division Duplex
    (FDMA-FDD), 4

G

General Authorized Access (GAA), 100

H

Heterogeneous networks
    (HetNet), 113
High speed packet access (HSPA), 5, 41
Hybrid Automatic Repeat Request
    (HARQ), 5

I, J, K

Inter-cell interference coordination
    (ICIC), 23
International Mobile Communications
    (IMT), 112
Internet of Things (IoT), 47, 82
Interoperability testing (IOT), 28, 47

L

Large scale parameters (LSP), 121
Licensed Shared Access (LSA), 43, 89
Link adaptation (LA), 30
Low-density parity check codes
    (LDPC), 129

© Intel Corp. 2016
B. Badic et al., *Rolling Out 5G*, DOI 10.1007/978-1-4842-1506-7

Get the eBook for only $5!

Why limit yourself?

Now you can take the weightless companion with you wherever you go and access your content on your PC, phone, tablet, or reader.

Since you've purchased this print book, we're happy to offer you the eBook in all 3 formats for just $5.

Convenient and fully searchable, the PDF version enables you to easily find and copy code—or perform examples by quickly toggling between instructions and applications. The MOBI format is ideal for your Kindle, while the ePUB can be utilized on a variety of mobile devices.

To learn more, go to www.apress.com/companion or contact support@apress.com.

Printed in the United States
By Bookmasters